How To Build A Cheap Chopper

Timothy Remus

Published by:
Wolfgang Publications Inc.
217 Second Street North
Stillwater, MN 55082
http://www.wolfgangpublications.com

Legals

First published in 2004 by Wolfgang Publications Inc.,
217 Second Street North, Stillwater MN 55082

ISBN number: 1-929133-17-0

Printed and bound in the USA

Cheap Chopper

Acknowledgements

Guest editors, what a cool idea. Somebody else does the writing and takes the photos and all I have to do is pay Jacki to put it all together. Of course it's never quite that easy (just ask Brian Klock), but I do have to thank all the individuals who contributed to this book. That list includes Steven Tersteeg, who not only built his own frame and then assembled his own motorcycle, but photographed the whole thing and even wrote the captions. Alan Mayes, editor of a very cool magazine called Ol' Skool Rodz, contributed the images and copy for Chapter Eleven, the E-Z Choppa sequence. I even have to thank the tardy Mr. Klock whose creative abilities extend well beyond his two-wheeled endeavors.

And for allowing me into their shop and enduring endless questions I would like to thank: Tom Summers of Lowriders by Summers, Frank Pedersen and crew from Motorcycle Works, and Dave Perewitz and his merry crew of very talented misfits.

Last, though certainly not least, thanks must be extended to Vince and Mike from Redneck Engineering, and ace mechanics Mikey and Tim.

Credit for layout goes to Jacki Mitchell. For in-house proof reading credit goes to Krista Leary.

In closing I tip my hat to my lovely and talented wife, Mary Lanz, who does proof reading, cooking and a variety of tasks I never seem to get around to, especially when it's deadline time.

Thanks to one and all, I pulled it off one more time.

Introduction

Call it a reaction to overpriced billet bikes with paint jobs that cost more than a used Buell. Call it a back-to-basics movement fueled by a growing number of individuals who think raw, flat black choppers with four-cylinder Japanese engines are cool as hell. Call it the end of boredom for owners of under-utilized Sportsters and Buells looking for a way to breath new life into an older motorcycle. Call it the answer to all the people who watch Monday night TV and desperately want a really cool big twin chopper with all the right stuff, but simply can't afford it.

Whatever the reasons, there are a whole pile of people interested in building or buying a Cheap Chopper.

What we've presented here are three basic types of cheap chopper: The metric ride, the Sportster/Buell ride and the big twin built from new aftermarket parts.

Unlike our earlier chopper book (How to Build A Chopper) this book uses over 60% of the pages for assembly sequences and the balance to discuss necessary topics like Brakes and Frames. There are seven sequences in all, some more complete than others. Everything from a ultra cheap Honda to a not-really-very-cheap big twin.

We've tried to cover everything from disassembling a used Buell to assembling the new bike. Ultimately there are a few things we left out. Like factory specifications for torque and clearances. Thus we recommend you buy a manual for the donor bike, or for a bike similar to the one you're building, i.e. a softail manual if you're building a complete aftermarket hardtail.

The bikes are cheap, the parts are available. What you don't know can be found in this book, at the local shop or on the web. The only thing we can't provide is will power. The only one who can get you up off your rear and out from in front of the TV is you.

No more excuses. Go build a motorcycle and ride the hell out of it.

Chapter One

History & Perspective

They Weren't all Big Twins in 1969

WHAT'S A CHOPPER

We all think we know exactly what a chopper is. Yet, if you ask five people to define a chopper you're likely to get five different answers. It might be easier to define what a chopper isn't. Choppers aren't dressers, they're not Dynas or Sportsters. For most people a chopper is a very simple bike with a certain attitude. Usually a long machine without rear suspension, without turn signals and with only the most essential sheet metal.

The property of Dave Cowan, this simple big twin chopper started life as a complete Hard-core kit from Custom Chrome. Not satisfied with the way the bike looked at mock-up, Dave turned to Bruce at Wizard Studios in Blaine, MN for help. Together they decided on more rake and a higher neck, (done at the Donnie Smith shop). Additional changes include a shortened fender, fabricated struts, a modified Sportster tank and scalloped paint.

Good Old Days

Though we tend to see the past through rose tinted glasses, those old days weren't always as good as we like to think. Yes, there were a lot of choppers on the road, and they were built with large doses of creativity and soul. But not all of them were good, usable motorcycles. At least some of those greasy old choppers were just that, greasy old motorcycles. Strip away the romance and you have an unreliable machine with marginal brakes and poor handling.

When you build that new chopper remember that it isn't 1969. You do want a disc brake on the front. You do want an engine that runs on a regular basis. You do want a bike that handles in a safe and predictable fashion. Unless you're an experienced rider you probably don't want a jockey shift (even if they do look really cool). The best motorcycles are those that can be ridden on a regular basis. Choppers are all about style, about making a statement. Don't however, let that thinking lead you to building a bike that sacrifices too much function in favor of form.

More History

We are currently enjoying a renaissance of Choppers. What you might call Chopper Craze Phaze Two. Part one of the craze ran from the late 1960s to the early 1980s. During part one, or at least the early

Sort of a big-twin Buell chopper, this hardtail seen at Redneck Engineering uses Buell wheels, front end assembly and even the little headlight fairing.

Buells make a great donor bike, but that doesn't mean you can't use a Sportster as the foundation for a nice inexpensive chopper. The owner of the 883 shown here is asking only $3900 for the 1999 bike.

stages of part one, a chopper could be built from almost any motorcycle imaginable. A Harley-Davidson, a Triumph or even a (gasp) Honda. By the end of the period however, choppers evolved into a tightly defined formula set in stone by a certain movie. A formula that included the long hardtail frame and Harley-Davidson big twin engine. No matter what the engine, choppers of the day were often built by combining a complete motorcycle with a frame from the Jammer or AEE catalog. Of course if the bike you started with was a stock hardtail Harley-Davidson, then there wasn't much need for an aftermarket frame.

By the time choppers came around for the second time in the late 1990s, builders had a wide range of aftermarket parts and engines to pick from. Instead of starting with an existing Sportster or Bonneville, the new-age builders could simply open a catalog and order a frame designed to accept a 250 rear tire, billet wheels with matching rotors, fat tires, a gas tank in almost any shape imaginable, and most important, complete aftermarket motors in displacements that start at 80 and top out at over 140 cubic inches.

There is only one problem with these craze-two bikes. While they may be immensely better, faster and even safer than those built thirty and more years ago, they cost more as well, even after you allow for inflation.

OLD SCHOOL THINKING

What to do? Why not do it the old-school way? Which is not to say you have to use a Maltese-cross mirror or a gold metal-flake paint job. By old-school we mean start with a donor

This clean Sportster is one of three from Big Bike, May of 1970. Also included were two Panheads, one Knuckle and one flathead trike. The readers' ride section included a Knuckle, an "English Indian," one Triumph and one Norton. A styling article suggested various chopper treatments for Honda 750s.

bike, minimize the number of aftermarket parts, use a large dose of creativity in place of expensive billet goodies, and skip the expensive paint job.

Instead of a long, exotic, expensive chopper, build a basic bike that's dependable, inexpensive, easy to ride and easy to maintain. Remember, the first choppers weren't built in elaborate shops. Most were assembled in the garage, the basement, spare bedroom or the living room.

Give up the idea that a chopper has to have a 124 cubic inch engine with show polish, a six-speed transmission and a 300 series rear tire. Start instead with a complete four-cylinder Honda (or a Kawasaki for that matter), or maybe a Sportster or Buell. Use the catalog from Drag Specialties or Custom Chrome like they used the one from Jammer in the old days: as a source for the frame, gas tank and only a few necessary accessories.

THE DONOR BIKE

A complete Sportster or Buell can be had for the price of an aftermarket engine – or less. Though prices seem to be creeping up, a used Buell can be had for three thousand and up. Old Hondas and their kin can often be found at swap meets or in the back of a garage for only a few hundred dollars. I recently saw a very nice late 1970s complete Kawasaki 1000 for only sixteen hundred dollars. Even big twins have come

Eric Buell didn't know he was designing a perfect chopper-donor bike. Buells come with more horsepower, better brakes, generally a more sophisticated front fork assembly, and wider wheels and tires - than a similar Sportster.

Ironhead Sportsters make great choppers. Be certain though that the engine and tranny are in good condition, as the bikes are getting to the point where parts (and good mechanics) are hard to find.

down in price. Complete Shovelheads (and even Evos) can now be found for five thousand and up.

Hardtail frames designed to accept a 750 Honda engine, built during the good old days, can often be found at swap meets or on the ever growling number of "chopper" web sites. There's currently enough interest in this emerging old-school way of doing things that a limited number of reputable shops are once again building new frames designed for the metric chopper market.

Only a year ago there were only a few companies in the aftermarket manufacturing frames for the Sportster/Buell drivetrain. Luckily, that situation has changed for the better. While there are still vastly more chopper frames manufactured for the big twin, a growing number of reputable companies are now building complete frames for Sportsters and Buells.

In fact, this phaze-two chopper phenomenon is a little bit like phaze one in reverse. When choppers first hit the streets in the late 1960s, Sportsters and metric bikes led the way. This time we started with big twins, and are only now seeing the acceptance of (and demand for) metric and Sportster-based choppers.

The assembly sequences seen farther along in this book include two inexpensive metric bikes, three fairly inexpensive Sportster/Buell based bikes and a somewhat expensive big twin "catalog" bike. What's expensive or inexpensive is up to you. For anyone working their way through school, a five thousand dollar metric bike might be expensive. For a lot of people though, the Sportster/Buell based bikes are pretty obtainable, especially if you already have the donor bike in the garage.

No longer can you complain that the bikes are

You don't have to use an Evo engine in your big twin chopper. The Shadley Brothers used a new B series T-C engine set in a short Rolling Thunder frame. The 41mm forks and billet wheels were purchased as overstock. Note the direct ignition (coils right on the plugs), a Shadley Bros. specialty, and the BDL belt drive.

too expensive or simply unobtainable. Prices are down, part are available. If you can't find what you want you just aren't looking hard enough.

DREAM BIKE

We all have a certain bike or a particular style of motorcycle that makes wood – that defines for us what a chopper should be. You need to know precisely what your new motorcycle is going to look like before you start. Don't just start collecting parts with the idea that somehow all that stuff will magically assemble itself into a running, usable motorcycle. Cut out pictures of your favorite bikes from the magazines or draw out what the ideal machine should look like. Now figure out how much money all those parts are going to cost. Then see if you can't get the dream bike and budget to overlap. It's important to know what you're going to build ahead of time and stick with that plan.

Deviations from that original concept cost both time and money. Time to take one part off and install another, or just re-think the whole deal. And buying a second set of forward controls, or fork tubes or whatever is simply more money out of pocket. Perhaps the worst part of changing the program in mid-stream is the lost momentum. Building a bike isn't rocket science but it is a big project, even if you're building a kit (more on kits later). Too

E-Z Choppa is part of the Bike In A Box program from Biker's Choice. For less than $15,000.00 you get a complete motorcycle with raised neck frame, 6 " over wide glide front end, 21/16 inch spoked wheels, 96 inch S&S motor, 5-speed tranny, all sheet metal, wiring and hardware. Biker's Choice

A very nifty Sportster-based chopper from Klock Werks, one of the first built with his new frame. Obviously Brian Klock doesn't know that Sportsters are for girls.

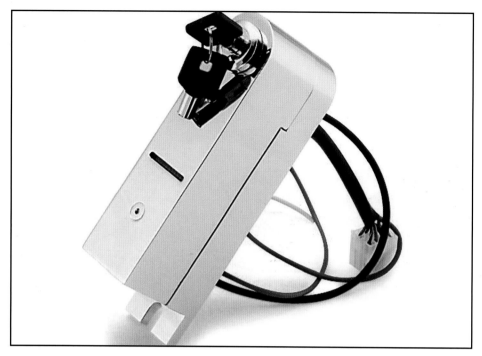

A whole host of harness kits and switch assemblies are available from those big catalogs, all designed to make wiring your chopper as easy and as clean as possible. Biker's Choice

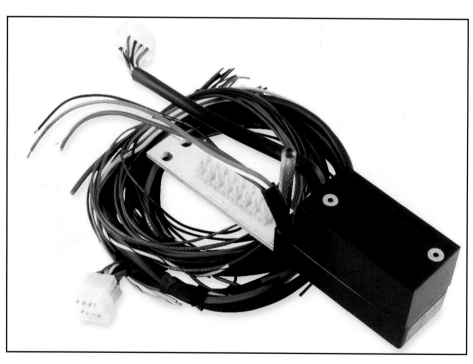

If you're not comfortable making up a harness from scratch, try a harness kit like this one from Wire Plus. Kits come with instructions and include built in diagnostic capability.

many projects end up as "basket case specials" for sale in the Sunday paper four year later. Don't built a basket. Know what you're going to build, stick with the plan and finish the project.

THE MONEY

How much does all this cost? In a very rough sense, a metric chopper can be built for less than five thousand dollars. A Sportster Buell bike will cost under ten thousand dollars and a big twin bike can be assembled for less than twenty thousand dollars. All these prices are approximate for a reason. No two bikes are going to be alike. All prices assume you do most of the labor, that you pass on the expensive billet goodies and the expensive paint job.

KITS

Kits, both complete and rolling chassis kits, have been on the scene for a number or years now. They offer a number of advantages, including the fact that you know ahead of time what the bike will look like, the fact that all the parts fit together, and the cost is nearly always less than if you bought the parts separately.

Custom Chrome, one of the first to offer complete bike kits, has their 2004 Hard Core for less than fourteen thousand dollars, complete with plain-finish 100 inch engine and six speed transmission. Though perhaps not a chopper, the

Nemesis kit is only about thirteen thousand dollars retail with soft-tail style chassis and natural-finish engine. The Goliath, with 250 rear and 21 inch front tire and hardtail frame is about seventeen thousand retail.

Biker's Choice offers it's own range of kits, including the E-Z Choppa, a complete bike kit featured in Chapter Ten.

And these are just the tip of the proverbial iceberg. There are more companies offering rolling chassis kits than there are flavors of ice cream at Baskin Robbins. As we said, the good thing about kits (besides the money) is the fact that you know what the profile of the bike will be ahead of time. The other really nice thing is the fact that you don't have to worry how long the fork tubes should be, or who you can get to weld on the mounts for the gas tank or rear fender.

OBSTACLES

Once you get past the biggest obstacle (money) the rest is relatively easy, though a few speed bumps do remain. Few of us have all the skills needed to completely assemble a bike. You may be a good mechanic but a lousy electrician, or a good painter but a poor assembler. The point is, most of us need help with at least a few of the necessary operations, so....

Don't be afraid to ask for help. Whether it's paint or wiring or upholstery, budget for a little help and don't assume it will come for free. Most service shops will help with wiring (or whatever) but you need to plan for this. That is, don't put the bike all together and then roll it into the local shop and ask them to "wire it." Ask them when you buy the kit or frame if they will help with the wiring, and then ask them at what stage of assembly they want you to bring it in.

KNOW YOUR SHOP

This piece of advice won't apply to all Cheap Chopper Builders, but we pass it along anyway. Find a good shop in your area and try to buy as much as possible at that one shop. You might be able to get the parts cheaper on the 'net, or mail order, but it's hard to get the person on the other end of the 800 number (assuming there is one) to wire the bike or help with driveline alignment or answer a very specific question about your particular machine. Most shops, especially small ones, are more than willing to help or answer questions, but you have to meet them halfway – support your local motorcycle shop.

Ultimately, it's up to you to decide what kind of chopper you really want and what you expect it to do. Now figure out a budget and start searching for parts. The following tips are sure to help you complete that dream bike project:

1. Just do it.
2. Keep doing it. Don't quit or get discouraged or change the style half way through.
3. See the project through to the very end.
4. Go ride.

A large number of rolling chassis kits are available in a wide variety of styles. This ProFat kit from Biker's Choice is based on a soft-tail chassis and can be ordered for either T-C or Evo engine. The nice thing is you know what the bike will look like, the sheet metal fits, and all the mounts are welded in place.

Chapter Two

Title & Insurance

Don't Underestimate the Paper Work

TITLE WORK

First things first. When you buy a frame, engine cases, or a complete engine from any legitimate aftermarket supplier you will get an MSO (Manufacturers' Statement of Origin). This paper work is essential if you want to get a title for your new motorcycle. Be sure MSOs are filled out correctly and that any previous transfers are noted. Before providing a title for any home-built bike most states insist that you provide

Whether or not you need full coverage depends both on how well you know your agent, and the amount of money you have in that new chopper. If it really is cheap, then you can likely get by with liability insurance.

them with the MSO with serial numbers noted for both the engine cases and the frame.

It goes without saying (though we always say it anyway): If the parts aren't clean, don't buy 'em. If the paper work seems funny, walk away. Because you don't need the hassle when it comes time to obtain a legal title, and you don't want to take a chance on supporting the people who might steal your motorcycle.

In the case of a complete bike built from aftermarket parts, the state will want to see receipts for all the parts you purchased to build the motorcycle. They want to know that the parts are legal and that applicable sales tax has been paid. Shops that go through this process on a regular basis suggest you keep a duplicate file of receipts and a photo record of the project as well. Many states require you to bring the finished bike to a DMV station or highway patrol officer for an inspection.

In the case of a donor bike mated with a new frame, you need the MSO for the new frame, and the title and bill of sale for the donor bike. In states that make the process easy, that's really all you need. As Brian Klock from Klock Werks explained, "In South Dakota, you take the title for your donor bike, and the MSO for the new frame to the DMV station.

The bike is titled as a rebuilt motor vehicle. If the new frame has a 17 digit VIN number they just assign that number to the new title. You don't even have to have an inspection."

Each state is a little different, so it pays to call and ask for the guidelines. Also be sure to

No. 3998

MANUFACTURERS' STATEMENT OF ORIGIN TO A MOTOR VEHICLE

The undersigned CORPORATION hereby certifies that the new motor vehicle described below, the property of said CORPORATION, has been transferred this 19th day of JUNE, 2003 on Invoice No. 619032 to:

John Doe
123 Main Street
Anywhere, USA 12345

Trade Name:
BAKER 6-Speed RSD Transmission

Year: 2003

Model: R701P

I.D. Number: DH118

The CORPORATION further certifies that this was the first transfer of such new motor vehicle in ordinary trade and commerce.

BAKER Incorporated
(Corporation)

By:_____ **President**

9804 E. Saginaw
Haslett, MI 48840
(Office Address of Signator)

Incorporated April 1998
State of Michigan

On a bike built completely from scratch (no donor bike) you are required to have an MSO only for the frame and engine. Most companies who sell transmissions provide only a receipt with the case numbers. Baker and a few others go the extra mile and provide an MSO for the transmission.

include all the items required for a motorcycle in your state, i.e. turn signals and horn. The best advice on getting through this process might come from shops that regularly build bikes and are forced to get good at working through the state's requirements. Ask them what's really need-ed. It might be a good idea to use the same DMV or inspection station that a busy shop does, simply because the people who work at that facility are accustomed to dealing with situations like yours.

**MANUFACTURER'S
STATEMENT OF ORIGIN
TO A MOTOR CYCLE FRAME**

The undersigned CORPORATION hereby certifies that the new motorcycle frame described below, the property of said MANUFACTURER, has been transferred this **23rd** day of **January, 2003 on invoice 2807.**

To: **American Thunder
16760 Toronto Ave. S.E.
Prior Lake, MN   USA
55372**

TYPE OF MOTORCYCLE FRAME

Style: **Softail – 250 (Right Side drive)**

Shipping Weight: **91 lbs. (ninety-one)**

Year Model: **2003**

Number: **2 R T M C 0 7 2 5 3 M**

The MANUFACTURER further certifies that this was the first transfer of such new motorcycle frame in ordinary trade and commerce.

Manufacturer: **Rolling Thunder Mfg. Inc.**

Signed by:

Bill Ford, Vice- President

Address: **1810 Ford Boulevard
Chateauguay, Quebec
J6J 4Z2 (Canada)**

Both frame and engine manufacturers provide an MSO

INSURANCE

Insurance becomes an issue because in most cases the new bike you build won't be titled as a Honda or a Harley-Davidson, but as a Redneck or a Santee. Insurance companies run by the "law of large numbers." There are lots of Harley-Davidsons on the street, val-ues are easy to calculate, acci-dent and theft trends can be documented. There aren't very many "Santee" or "Perewitz" or "Motorcycle Works" motorcycles out there. This scares the hell out of the insurance companies because of the unknowns. How do they determine a value, how often do these bikes fall down or disappear?

If you ask ten people from the motorcycle industry how they deal with this, nine give the same answer. "It all depends on the person buy-ing the insurance and their agent or company. If you have the house, business, boat and car all with the same company and now you want insurance for this bike you built, they have an incentive to provide the insurance. But otherwise, they only want to sell you liability, they don't want to cover the bike."

To quote Brian Klock again, "If you have all your insurance with one company, then they will sometimes write a full coverage policy on the bike. You have a little leverage. In those cases I usually have to do an appraisal of the bike's value and list the parts we used and any hand made parts, and include a photo file that they can go back to if there is an accident. But if you're a kid living in a trailer you're going to pay a lot."

MONEY TO LEND

Bankers are at least as risk-averse as the guys who run big insurance companies. If you need to borrow money for this project it's going to be far easier to borrow against the donor bike, even if the value is marginal, than against a pile of parts or the idea of building a bike from scratch.

Option number two is to borrow against the house (tax deductible) or another large asset that has untapped equity. If the project is cheap enough you might be tempted to pay as you go. Just buy the bike, buy the new frame and start screwing the two together. The problem comes when the bike, or frame, or accessories, or outside labor go over budget. If you run out of money to buy the parts, progress on the bike stops. Lost inertia follows. Pretty soon a full year has passed and the new chopper is nothing more than a bunch of junk cluttering up one corner of the garage.

Know ahead of time how much it's going to cost to build the bike and where that money is going to come from. When you do the budget (before starting on the bike) include a fudge factor to cover those Murphy's Law situations that always develop.

FIRST ASSIGNMENT

FOR VALUE RECEIVED, the undersigned hereby transfers this **Statement of Origin** and the motor vehicle described therein to _____
Address _____
_____,
and certifies that the vehicle is new and has not been registered in this or any other state; he also warrants the title of said motor vehicle at time of delivery, subject to the liens and encumbrances, if any, as set out below.

Amt of Lien	Date	To Whom Due	Address

Date _____, at _____

American Thunder By: _(Sign Here)_ _(Position)_
Transferor (Firm Name)

SECOND ASSIGNMENT

FOR VALUE RECEIVED, the undersigned hereby transfers this **Statement of Origin** and the motor vehicle described therein to _____
Address _____
_____,
and certifies that the vehicle is new and has not been registered in this or any other state; he also warrants the title of said motor vehicle at time of delivery, subject to the liens and encumbrances, if any, as set out below.

Amt of Lien	Date	To Whom Due	Address

Date _____, at _____

_____ By: _____
Transferor (Firm Name)　　　　(Sign Here)　　　(Position)

THIRD ASSIGNMENT

FOR VALUE RECEIVED, the undersigned hereby transfers this **Statement of Origin** and the motor vehicle described therein to _____
Address _____
_____,
and certifies that the vehicle is new and has not been registered in this or any other state; he also warrants the title of said motor vehicle at time of delivery, subject to the liens and encumbrances, if any, as set out below.

Amt of Lien	Date	To Whom Due	Address

Date _____, at _____

_____ By: _____
Transferor (Firm Name)　　　　(Sign Here)　　　(Position)

The back side of a MSO is laid out much like a title card, with space to note each legal transfer. Be sure all transfers are duly noted and that all your paper work is super clean.

Chapter Three

Frames and Frame Geometry

Achieve Good Looks *and* Good Handling

Frank Pedersen from Motorcycle Works in Olathe, Kansas (just south of Kansas City if you're wondering) likes to compare the motorcycle frame with the foundation of a house. "If you are building a house and the foundation is crooked you are fighting it all the way through. But if the foundation is good then the whole job goes well."

So take Frank's advice and buy a good one. By good we mean a frame that's straight, with all

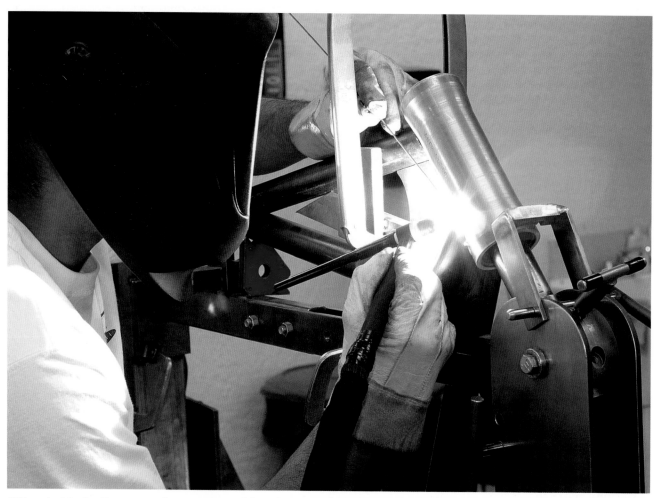

What holds the frame together are the welds, which should be done by qualified personnel using tig-welders. Precise mitered joints require less filling and less heat - resulting in stronger joints and less warpage.

the brackets welded on in the right locations. A frame that won't require a lot of shims or enlarged holes to correctly locate the major components. No less an authority than Donnie Smith commented that, "People try to save money when they buy the frame, but it always ends up costing them more in the long run."

The best judge of good and bad frames are the guys and gals who use them day after day. People who build motorcycles on a regular basis. If the frames aren't straight, if the drivetrain doesn't line up easily, these are the people who know.

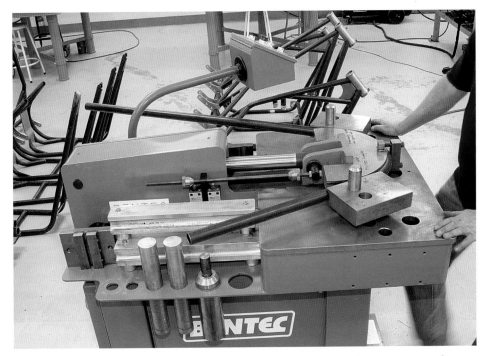

Before you can build consistent frames you need consistent bends, provided in this case by the hydraulic tubing bender at Fabrication Plus (home of Arlen Ness Frames).

THE FRAME JIG

Building a quality frame requires a stout jig to hold all the components in the correct relationship to each other – on every frame every time. Because most frames are constructed from round tubing, each junction requires a mitered cut. Seldom do the two pieces of tubing come together at exactly 90 degrees, which means the beveled joint is a complex shape. Some companies use a fixture and a Bridgeport mill to precisely cut these mitered joints, at least the big ones where the top tube and down tubes meet the neck. There are even "miter boxes" designed to cut concave miters of various sizes and angles from steel tub-

Once the tubing is bent, it needs to be clamped into a quality jig. At Fabrication Plus the frame jigs are built in-house starting with heavy surface plates and quality clamps and fixtures.

ing, fancy laser cutters are also available for fabrication shops that can justify the expense. Commonly though the cuts are done with a hand grinder, which is fine if the fabricator is careful about the fit between the two pieces of tubing.

The long-winded explanation is necessary because of the fact that heat moves metal. And loose joints require more filler material which requires more heat which means more movement of the metal during the welding operation(s). All of which comes back to the fact that some frames are better than others, it's up to you to find a good one. (See Frank Pedersen's interview in Chapter Seven for more on frame manufacture.)

DEFINITIONS

Before delving further into a discussion of frames it might be helpful to define some terms. Rake is the angle of the fork assembly as compared to vertical. With choppers the rake at the neck may be different than the rake of the fork, this discrepancy is done in order to achieve the best figure for trail.

Trail is the distance between the front tire's contact patch and the point where the centerline of the bike's steering axis meets the ground (see the illustrations). Motorcycles have positive trail. Much like the caster angle of an automobile, positive trail provides the straight line stability that allows us to take our hands off the bars while going down the road.

Most motorcycle designers and builders like trail figures in the four to six inch range. Most factory bikes fall into this same range. In fact, the chart for the current model line up from Milwaukee lists trail figures from 4.1 to 6.2 inches. In general, sport bikes run less trail which tends to make them quicker to change direction (some would call it twitchy) while cruisers and factory customs run more.

With most standard-issue front fork assemblies and standard triple trees an increase in rake will result in an increase in positive trail. With choppers this means a rake angle of 45 degrees can result in a trail dimension of eight or more inches. Too much trail means great straight line stability, but a lot of what's called "flop" at slow speeds, a front end that wants to fall into the turn.

The trail dimension can be altered without altering the frame, with the use of "raked trees." (Check the illustrations here for clarification.) In fact, some of the factory bikes from Milwaukee use raked trees to help them achieve what the engineers consider an ideal figure. Before bolting a set of raked trees on your bike remember that raked trees reduce trail. Exactly how much depends on the angle and

A special cutting tool in the Bridgeport and matching fixture insure a very precise mitered cut. Good fitment between individual pieces of tubing mean consistent dimensions, and no need for extra filler or additional heat when the parts are welded together.

height of the neck, the size of the front wheel and where the triple trees position the fork tubes relative to the neck.

Don't skip ahead here - this is important stuff. Because raked trees reduce trail you can't just bolt a set of seven-degree trees to a stock Sportster to give it that long raked look. Raked trees on a stock bike can easily move the machine into a negative trail situation. This means that instead of falling into a turn as some bikes with excessive trail do, the bike will simply fall over instead. We're talking major instability here.

Experienced chopper builders might buy a frame with 40 degrees of rake and then use a set of "five-degree trees" (this is an example, don't duplicate these numbers) for a total of 45 degrees of rake. By using the five-degree trees they reduce the trail to a more manageable level (approximately four inches) and get rid of that really heavy feeling, most noticeable on slow speed turns, that results from extreme trail dimensions.

What all this means is that you have to buy a rolling chassis kit from a quality manufacturer who has already figured out the trail, or carefully determine the trail for yourself. There are some web sites that have trail calculators, see the nearby side-bar for more.

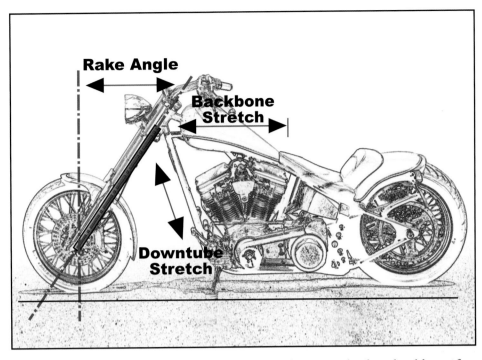

When people talk about stretch, they should specify whether they're talking about the backbone or downtubes. Sometimes people just say a particular frame is "four up and three out."

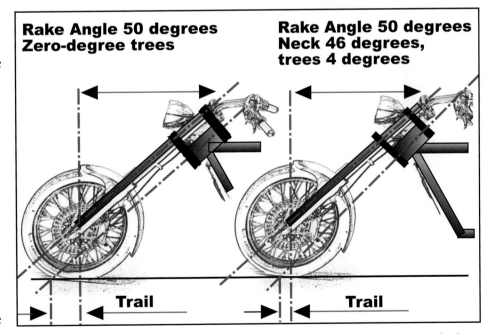

When you get to "chopper" rake angles you also get to high trail figures. Which is why most experienced builders use raked trees - to reduce the trail to a more manageable figure. Be careful though before using raked trees on a stock frame, as you might end up with little or no positive trail.

On the Trail to Stability

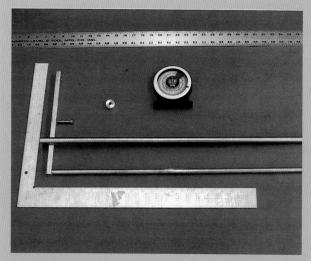

Trail checking tool kit. The carpenter's square and protractor came from the lumber store, the rest of the tool was fabricated from various pieces of aluminum stock.

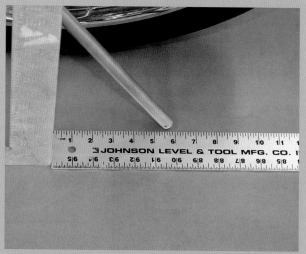

Even with only about 34 degrees of rake this bike comes in at nearly 6 inches of trail. We checked another bike (not shown) with a 34 degree neck and came up with 6 inches as well.

This is the basic set up. The small cross shaft bolts to the bottom of the lower triple tree. Aluminum tubing (the pointer) slides over a slightly smaller piece of aluminum stock.

Protractor with a magnetic base is available from most lumber and hardware stores.

On the Trail to Stability

The best way to know for sure what the trail is on that new chassis you just purchased is to check it. Option number two (and a good aid to planning a chassis) is to use the very slick trail calculator at perseperformance.com. RB Racing also has a calculator at: www.rbracing-rsr.com/rake-andtrail.html. And if that's not enough, there's a rake/trail/tube length chart in the Drag Specialties catalog.

Back to the photos on these two pages. The shop images come from American Thunder in Prior Lake, Minnesota (a certified Wolfgang Publications affiliate shop). The trail-checking tool is a simple little tool that Neal and crew assembled from aluminum stock - designed to screw into the threaded hole found in the bottom of most triple trees.

As you can see, there's lot of difference between a bike with a 33 degree neck and another with a 40 degree neck. Vince from Redneck Engineering likes to see the trail between three and five inches, the Perse Website uses a figure of 3.5 to 5 inches. Some stock Harley-Davidsons come with six inches however, so maybe that should be the upper limit.

The important thing is to be aware of the impact that trail has on the bike's handling, and avoid building a bike that falls outside what most chassis experts and professionals consider to be the acceptable range.

The protractor on this frame reads 40 degrees, meaning we likely have more trail than with the 35 degree frame (though height of neck, wheel diameter and even the distance from the centerline of the neck to the centerline of the tubes affect the trail).

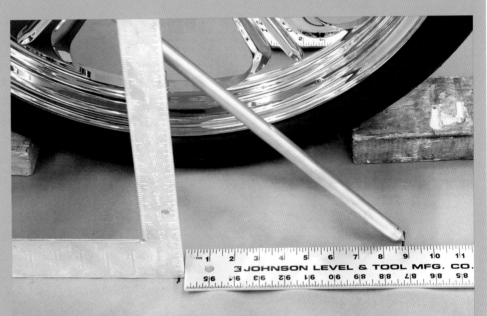

And we do have more trail, nearly nine inches total which is well outside the "four to six" guideline quoted by most builders.

Prior to paint, this is one of the Mutant Buell frames from Redneck Engineering, manufactured from DOM tubing and tig welded.

This Sportster rigid frame from Paughco is designed for '86 to '01 engines, comes with no stretch, an extra 5 degrees of rake and sells for a little over $600.

Designed for 4-speed tranny with Evo or pre-Evo engine, this Easy Rider style wishbone frame from Paughco sells for less than $800.

STRETCH

There are two types of "stretch." Typical stretch refers to material added to the top tube – sometimes called a stretched backbone. Downtube stretch refers to the material added to the downtubes to raise the neck. On the street people say a certain frame is "four inches ahead and three inches up," meaning the neck is positioned four inches ahead and three inches higher than a "stock" frame.

THE LOOK

Frame dimensions are very important for a number of reasons. For one thing, the motorcycle frame needs to fit your frame. Big people are going to want more stretch and possibly a taller neck. Put a short person on a bike with a raised neck and they won't be able to see past the front of the gas tank and the upper triple tree.

You need to do more than just reach the controls and put you feet flat on the ground at a stop. The bike should be comfortable enough to ride, if not all the way to Sturgis, then at least for most of the day. Some corrections can be made with different bars and risers, but the basic chassis size, seat and bar positions all need to be situated to match your inseam and riding style.

Frame dimensions are important for another important reason. The dimensions of the frame (and to a lesser degree, the shape of the tank) go a long way toward determining the "look" or silhouette of the motorcycle. While all the bikes we're discussing are choppers, they don't all have the same appearance. There's a hell of a difference between a short stubby chopper with a dropped neck, and a long stretched chopper with raised neck.

So figure out which are the choppers you like the most, and roughly what their dimensions are. Now look for a frame or rolling chassis kit with those same dimensions.

Brian Klock suggests you keep a photo file, or clip images from magazines. When the pile gets to a suitable size, sort out the bikes you really like the best. Now figure out what it is that those bikes have in common, and what their likely frame dimensions are.

A CONVERSATION WITH VINCE DOLL OF REDNECK ENGINEERING

What started as a very small motorcycle shop only a few years ago has evolved into a sprawling fabrication facility responsible for the manufacture of over 1000 frames per year, and an undisclosed number of chassis kits and turn key custom bikes. The creation of Vince Doll, Redneck is like a hungry growing animal, always looking for more space to house more welders, fabricators and frame jigs. Follow along as Vince tells us how he feels about rake, trail and raised necks.

Vince, how long have you been making motorcycle frames?

Three and a half years.

How does a guy without much background in Motorcycles have so much success in such a short period of time?

My whole goal was to build stuff anyone could afford. We got aligned with people who treated us right and could help us build a good product at a very reasonable price. Our stuff isn't really cheap. Our fit and finish is very good. It takes no more time to do something right. For example, it actually takes less time to run the wires through the frame than to run them on the outside.

Tell us a little about how the Sportster/Buell frames came about?

For my first project I wanted to build a Sportster frame for the guy who was left out, a guy with an old Sportster in the garage. But we did a big twin frame first. And the first time we displayed that frame, at Biketoberfest in 2000, we sold 185,000 dollars worth. We were so busy after that we couldn't back up and get to the Sporty chassis. So it wasn't until Sturgis in 2003 that we debuted the first Sportster/Buell bike, the one that Mike Marquart built.

How is your frame different than some of the other Sportster frames on the market?

Most people start with a big twin frame and then put a sporty engine in it. We actually took tubing and built a frame around a Sportster engine. My initial idea was to give Sportster guys something to do with the bike they had in the garage, but when we built the first frame we had a Buell in the corner.

The factory doesn't set the engine in exactly the center of the frame, so we put a Sportster motor on a piece of angle iron until we found the exact center of balance. Then we marked the cases so we could set the motor right in the middle of the frame. Our new frames are perfectly balanced and will still accept a 200 rear tire.

How hard is it to title a bike built from a Redneck frame and a donor Buell or Sportster?

We give them an MSO, and they also need the title to the bike the engine came out of. In most states it ends up being titled as a re-construction bike.

What about insurance, how much of a hassle is it?

It depends mostly on the individual and their relationship with their insurance company. Some guys do it for $400 per year and some are spending $2000 for the same coverage. Because these bikes are so inexpensive, you might want to just run liability coverage and leave it at that.

Frame dimensions, what's safe and what's not. Everybody wants these extreme choppers, when do they become unstable, What do you like to see for rake and trail?

We won't go over eight up on a chopper and seven out. We prefer to see the rake at 42 to 44 degrees. Then we work with the trees to get the correct trail. A good riding bike is six to eight inches up, Eight is cool for a big guy. I like to see the trail at three to five inches. I try to put them at 4 inches.

On our springers we change the length of the rockers depending on the rake, that way we get the right amount of trail for a certain rake angle.

Vince Doll, always working to bring more hot rod motorcycles to more people for less money.

Chapter Four

Brakes

You Need to Whoa as well as Go

DEFINITIONS AND DIFFERENCES

Brakes come in two primary flavors, drum and disc. Drum brakes wouldn't even be part of this discussion except for our concept of the donor bike. The fact is, some of those donor bikes might be old enough to have drum brakes, especially on the rear.

A drum brake slows the bike by expanding two brake shoes out against the inside surface of the spinning drum, a disc brake on the other

If you're going too cut loose with some bucks for wheels and tires, take the time to match the rotor to the wheel, and be sure the finish (chrome in this case) is the same for wheel, caliper and lower legs.

hand squeezes the spinning disc between the brake pads. From a design standpoint, drum brakes suffer from at least three design flaws, flaws eliminated in the disc design. First, drum brakes are heavier than a disc brake having the same stopping power. Second, a overheated drum brake is slower to cool than a disc brake which by definition has the disc right out there in the air stream. Third, the drum lacks the self-cleaning abilities of a disc brake. Debris or oil that gets inside the drum can't get out. A disc by contrast tends to throw off any contaminants, a nice self-cleaning feature.

A huge selection of brake calipers are available, including these 4-piston designs from Hog Halters. Most calipers can be used on either the front or rear. Front mounts are pretty universal...

DON'T SKIMP

It's always tempting to skimp, especially when building what are essentially budget bikes. Yes, the old wiring harness can often be used, and an engine that uses just a little oil can be tolerated without much trouble. The one place where you don't want to skimp however, is on the brakes. You gotta have brakes, good brakes, or you're just looking for trouble. When it comes to planning that bike and deciding which parts can be re-used and how they should be installed, consider the following rules:

1) Always use a brake on the front wheel. Sure, some of those magazine bikes from 1972 didn't and

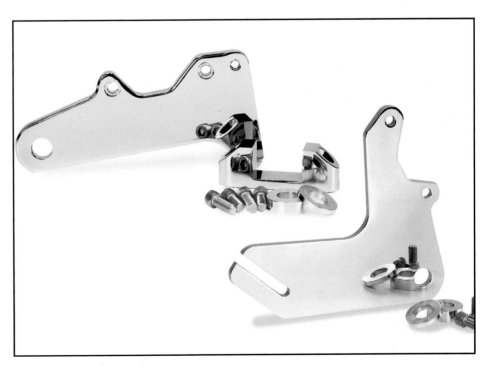

...thought rear mounts come in different styles and need to matched up to the frame during the mock-up. Biker's Choice

Hydraulic Ratios

Before buying a new Master Cylinder from Performance Machine and plumbing it to the stock factory Caliper from that 1996 Sportster you have to consider the hydraulic ratio between the two components.

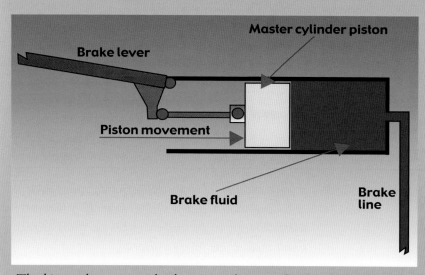

The bigger the master cylinder piston the more fluid is displaced. As the piston size grows however the amount of pressure (all other things being equal) goes down. Output is also affected by the lever ratio, which is why some metric masters have adjustable pivots.

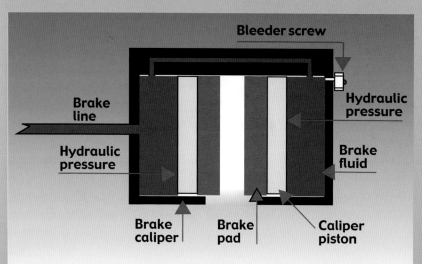

The force created in the master cylinder is transferred fully to the caliper pistons. The more piston area the more net force is created by a certain pressure. The trade off: more pistons (or calipers) require more volume to move all those pistons. That's why the diameter of the master cylinder piston is so important.

To explain hydraulic ratios we have to re-visit high school physics. It all comes down to one formula: Pressure = Force/Area. So if you put ten pounds of force on a master cylinder piston with one square inch of area, you have created a pressure of 10psi. If you change the master cylinder to a design with only 1/2 square inch of piston area, then you've created twice the pressure. The important part isn't just the 10psi of pressure, it's how that 10psi of pressure is utilized by the caliper.

If the caliper in question uses one piston with one square inch of piston area the force on the brake pad will be 10 pounds (Force = Pressure X Area). If you double the piston area you also double the force on the brake pad. After only a moment's consideration you realize that the way to achieve maximum braking force is with a small master cylinder piston working multiple caliper pistons with relatively high total area.

Remember though that everything has a price (no free lunch, ever). Small master cylinder pistons don't displace much liquid, and may not fully extend the caliper pistons. Matching up the best components is a matter of balance then, between pressure and volume.

If you're buying a complete new set up for the front wheel of that chopper, ask the sales person to recommend which master cylinder (they come with various piston sizes) to use with that four-piston caliper. If instead, you're mating a new master cylinder to an existing caliper, buy one with the same diameter piston as that used on the donor bike.

they looked cool and seemed to survive, but it remains a stupid thing to do. Because of weight transfer the front wheel does at least 70% of the stopping on a hard stop. Old timers always say, "choppers put most of the weight on the rear wheel so the front brake isn't as important." But consider that bikes with less rake and shorter forks don't really shift the weight bias all that much, and even if the ratio of front wheel power shifts to the point where it only accounts for 50% of the stopping, would you want to throw away half your braking power in that elusive search for a "clean looking" front wheel?

For all the above reasons the brake you use on the front wheel should be of the disc variety. And though builders of thirty years ago often used tiny discs and calipers for more of that certain sanitary look, you should not emulate the behavior. Choppers are all about style, yet tiny calipers, sometimes meant for go karts and such, don't have the power to stop a speeding motorcycle, especially when the disc they're squeezing is so small in diameter that the caliper doesn't have any leverage.

2) Carefully inspect all the used parts that will make up the brake system on the new bike. When in any doubt replace any suspect parts with new or rebuilt components. This includes obvious things like the brake pads and shoes, and the less obvious components like flexible line and calipers. If the piston(s) in the caliper doesn't slide easily back into the bore, take it apart, clean everything including any sliding pins and replace all the seals. If you haven't performed this operation before you might want to take the caliper down to the local

Honda or Harley shop and pay to have it done. Any flexible lines that show signs of wear and weather-checking should be replaced with new parts. Banjo bolts use a soft sealing washer on either side of the fitting. It's a good idea to replace these washers if you re-use any of the old hoses and lines.

3) On a hard stop the pressure in the hydraulic system goes to 1000psi and more. This means you can't use anything to carry the brake fluid except line and hoses designed and approved for use in a brake system. Whether it's factory-style black flexible hoses or trick braided aftermarket line, use hoses designed and approved for use on brake systems. Don't get creative here and pick up some hose from the hardware store because it's Sunday night and the motorcycle or parts store is closed. Use the right stuff.

We should note that some aftermarket brake hoses aren't DOT (Department of Transportation) approved, which doesn't mean they're bad, but could be a problem in states with tough inspection laws.

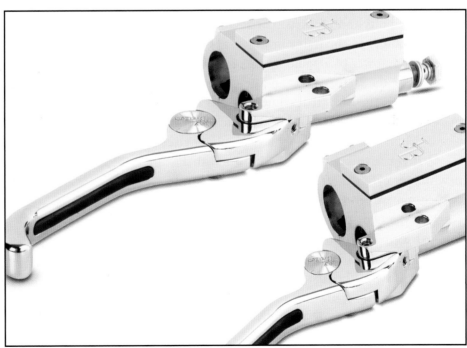

These master cylinders from JayBrake come with 5/8 or 3/4 inch pistons to better match the number of pistons and size used on the front caliper(s). Levers are also adjustable to accommodate both large and small hands. Biker's Choice

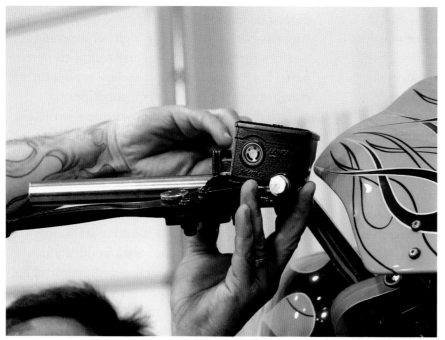

Using the components from the donor bike has a couple of advantages. First of course, it saves money. Second, you know the components are correctly matched.

BLEED THE BRAKES

Bleeding brakes is simply a matter of bleeding the air out of the system so there's nothing but liquid brake fluid in the system. But first a discussion of hydraulics.

Brakes follow hydraulic laws. These laws include the fact that a fluid can't be compressed to a smaller volume. Thus any and all pressure created by the piston in the master cylinder is delivered to the piston(s) in the caliper. Unlike liquids, gasses (like air) can be compressed to a smaller volume. Any air left in the lines or caliper after bleeding will be

4) There are at least two types of brake fluid (more in the nearby side-bar). Use one or the other and don't mix the two.

5) The bolts and brackets that anchor the drum or caliper to the frame or fork transfer all the braking power of a panic stop to the bike's chassis. Use the factory bolts and brackets whenever possible, the bolts that come with any aftermarket calipers you buy, and heavy brackets and Grade 8 bolts when you don't have anything else.

6) If you're mixing an OEM caliper with a new master cylinder, or buying new master and caliper, remember to consider the hydraulic ratios between the two components (see the nearby side-bar for more on these ratios).

7) New pads take time to seat on the rotors, so take it easy on the first few stops. After bleeding the system hold pressure on the lever and check all the connections carefully for leaks.

8) And though it sounds obvious, be sure to leave enough flex in the hoses so they aren't stretched tight during up and down suspension movement. Likewise be sure they can't rub on the tire or be pinched in any way.

If in doubt about the old brake pads, install new ones. Be sure the caliper pistons can be easily pushed back into the caliper - or have the caliper overhauled. To ensure a good seal, it's a good idea to replace the soft washers used on the banjo bolts.

Brake Fluid

Not all brake fluids are created equal and not all are compatible. There are three grades of brake fluid commonly available: DOT 3, DOT 4 and DOT 5. DOT 3 and 4 are glycol-based fluids and though these 4 fluids are often used in automobiles, you might not want to use them in your motorcycle because they absorb water from the environment and they attack most paints.

DOT 5 fluid, by contrast, is silicone based, meaning a higher boiling point, no tendency to absorb water and no reaction when spilled on a painted surface. It costs more and is reputed to be slightly compressible, though street riders never seem to notice any difference in feel or effect.

New Harley-Davidsons have used silicone-based fluid since the early 1980s and the fluid you will find on the shelf of the dealership or quality aftermarket shop is probably DOT 5.

No matter what you use, remember that the two types are not compatible and should never be mixed. This means you need to use the same fluid used in the donor bike when new – or flush the old fluid out of the donor bike's components. Given the fact that the donor bike components are used, the flushing is probably a good idea regardless of the original fluid used in that system.

The local auto-parts store will likely carry more than one type of brake fluid. Most custom builders prefer the silicone fluid.

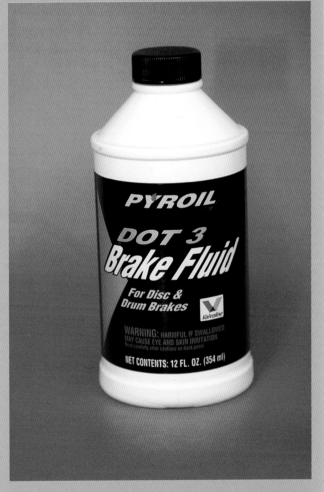

There's nothing wrong with Dot 3 and 4 brake fluid, except that it attacks any paint it comes into contact with.

Nothing's simple. Brake pads come in different materials, try to match the pad material to the rotor. Soft Kevlar-type pads work well with relatively soft cast iron rotors, sintered iron may be a better choice for stainless rotors. A knowledgeable counter person can often help with the selection.

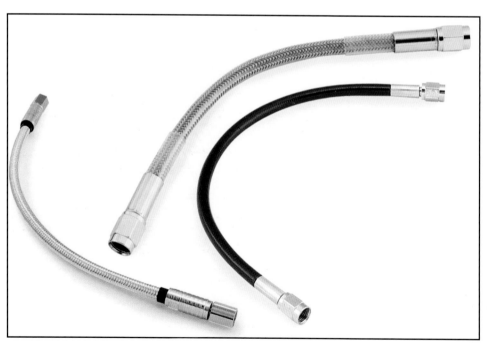

Flexible brake hoses (rated for use in brake systems) come in different styles. Some are DOT rated though many are not. Those wrapped in stainless braid may be covered in clear plastic, which prevents the stainless from cutting through the paint on the fender or swingarm.

compressed when you activate the lever or pedal, resulting in a mushy feeling lever and piss-poor brake performance.

Bleeding automotive brakes is often easier than a motorcycle because the master cylinder is bigger and moves a large volume of fluid with each stroke. You need a friend to pump the pedal two or three times and hold it down while you open the bleeder valve. With pressure on the system you open the valve, a frothy mixture of air and fluid comes out, you close the valve, and then your helper allows the pedal to come up so the process can be repeated over again. Bleeding goes on until nothing but pure, clean brake fluid exits the bleeder each time it's opened. Note, this only works if the bleeder is at the top of the caliper where the air bubbles congregate.

You can bleed the brakes on that new chopper in the time-honored process outlined above. It might be easier however, to use an EZ Bleeder type of system. In this scenario, you force fluid in at the bleeder with a fluid filler syringe until all the air is forced out of the system and pure fluid fills the master cylinder reservoir. If the bleeder valve ends up at the bottom of the caliper, you may have to take the caliper off the mount, put something between the pads and hold it "upside down" while the air out of the system.

If you have trouble getting a solid-feeling lever, don't feel like the Lone Ranger. Though simple in concept, bleeding bike brakes often turns out to be more hassle than you originally bargained for. Many shops have pressure bleeders that make the job easier, so when all else fails ask for help. Run the bike down to the local shop and ask their help in getting the last of the air out of those brake lines.

Motorcycles have a few unique problems in addition to the small master cylinder piston. Some handle bars, for example, position the master cylinder so the outlet is higher than the lever end, which means a bubble can become "lodged" at the outlet end. The solution is to somehow change the angle of the master cylinder (or take it off the bars) during the bleeding operation.

Banjo fittings, used on many calipers and master cylinders, come in a wide variety of shapes and styles to make neat routing of the brake lines as easy as possible. Biker's Choice

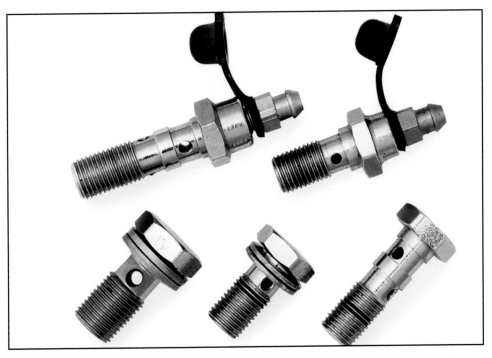

Banjo bolts are available in a wide range of styles as well, including some with integral bleeder screws. Biker's Choice

33

Chapter Five

Fasteners

Nuts 'n Bolts 101

THE BASIC BOLT

A bolt is nothing more than a threaded fastener designed to screw into a hole or nut with matching female threads. What follows is a very condensed explanation of fasteners, a topic about which many books have been written.

MANUFACTURE

Quality bolts are made in a rolling or forming operation. The raw stock, known as "wire," is rolled through special dies that form the threads

They aren't just nuts and bolts. These are the fasteners that hold your motorcycle together. In addition to their functional importance, good fasteners elevate the detail level of the bike.

without any cutting. Rolling threads encourages the grain to flow with the threads. Rolling the threads also compresses or forges the surface of the threads making them much stronger and leaves a smooth polished surface. While American or unified bolts are described as having 24 or 18 threads per inch, the metric system describes a bolt as having a pitch of a certain dimension, like 1.0 mm.

Grading Systems And Specifications
Thread Specifications in the Real World.

What we often call NC and NF or national course and national fine, are actually UNC and UNF. Or unified national course and unified national fine. This "unified" system came about after WW II and combined the best of the then-current American and English standards.

The specifications call for an included angle of 60 degrees for both the coarse and fine threaded fasteners, all of which are measured in the well known inch system.

There has been some evolution of the thread specifications since those first standards were written, but most of those have to do with the radius at the base of the thread. Without getting too deep, a sharp V-shaped notch at the base of the threads makes an ideal stress riser - a spot where the bolt is likely to fatigue and break.

There was enough room in the original specifications for a improvement in the shape of the threads. You can extend the fatigue life of a fastener by simply "rounding" the root, or base of the threads. Obviously this rounding, specified as a particular radius, eliminates the stress risers found in a pure V shape. Most of the better

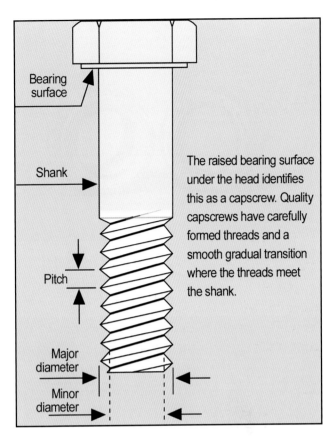

Bearing surface

Shank

Pitch

Major diameter

Minor diameter

The raised bearing surface under the head identifies this as a capscrew. Quality capscrews have carefully formed threads and a smooth gradual transition where the threads meet the shank.

The major parts of a fastener, note the bearing surface under the head of a true capscrew.

The radial lines indicate the Grade of a SAE bolt: three lines = Grade 5, six lines = Grade 8.

Skip the lock washers, use a ny-lock type lock nut instead, available in chrome and stainless.

Chrome Allen bolts look great, though you have to ask the vendor what grade they are, and understand their limitations.

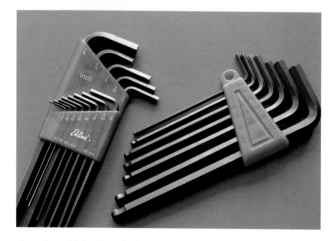

Speaking of Allen bolts, or SHCSs, you need at least one set of Allen wrenches, available with a ball head (a nice option) and in 3/8 inch drive.

bolts and capscrews (including SAE Grade 8) now specify an "R" thread which simply spells out the specific radius at the bottom of the thread.

The SAE Grading System

Most bike builders are familiar with SAE graded fasteners. These are the well-known Grade 5 and Grade 8 bolts we get from Gardner Wescott, the local industrial supply house or the local hardware store. SAE bolts come in various strengths. These bolts carry the radial dashes on the head that most of us have learned to identify. Three dashes is a Grade 5, while six identify the bolt as a Grade 8, a bolt many of us consider "as good as it gets."

Bolts are measured in pounds per square inch of tension or stress. The ultimate tensile strength, or UTS, is the point at which the bolt breaks. The other specification given for quality bolts is the yield point, or point at which the bolt will no longer bounce back to its original dimension once the stress is removed.

An SAE Grade 2 bolt, often called a hardware-store bolt, is rated at 74,000 psi UTS up to a size of 3/4 inch. This same bolt has a yield strength of 57,000 psi. Moving up the scale, a Grade 5 bolt, the point at which good bolts start, is rated at 120,000 psi UTS, and has a published yield point of 92,000 psi. Grade 5 bolts are considered good enough for most general purpose automotive and motorcycle use. What many of us consider the ultimate bolt, the Grade 8 bolt, is rated at 150,000 psi and 130,000 psi yield strength. Quality Grade 5 and 8 bolts have a manufacturer's marking on the head along with the radial dashes. This makes it easier to trace the bolt back to the manufacturer.

Metric Strength

On the metric side of the aisle, the strength of a bolt is indicated with a two or three-digit number on the head. Though they indicate newtons per square millimeter, the numbers can be converted to the more common SAE system as follows. An 8.8 is roughly equivalent to a Grade 5, while 10.9 is roughly equal to a Grade 8.

NUTS

A bolt isn't any good without matching female threads. Those threads commonly take the form of a nut, or threads tapped into a casting. In the case of a capscrew and nut, the strongest union is provided if the male and female components have fine threads (all other factors being equal), because this way you get a larger root diameter, and there is more physical contact between the threads.

The threads cut into a casting however, are often coarse, as coarse threads are better suited to those "coarse" materials and help to compensate for the difference in strength between the material the bolt is manufactured from and the material the casting is made from.

Nuts break down into self-locking and free-running. Generally there isn't a good reason not to use a good self-locking nut. These self locking nuts are especially helpful when screwing on semi-fragile parts, like fiberglass fenders, where you don't want the bolts terribly tight for fear of cracking the 'glass.

One of the most common self locking nuts is the ny-lock type of lock-nut that combines a six-point nut with a nylon collar. The nylon collar has no threads, so as the nut is screwed onto the bolt the bolt threads must force (but not cut) their way through the collar, which is sized to have an I.D. slightly smaller than the major diameter of the bolt. As the bolt threads its way through the nylon, friction is created between the metal male and female threads. Added to this is the friction between the nylon collar

and the bolt threads. The combination works well and resists vibration as well as anything else.

Nylon-collar nuts are available in chrome and stainless and can be reused. What these lock-nuts aren't good at is enduring high heat situations. For securing exhaust flanges and the like, a better choice is an all-metal lock nut.

ALLEN BOLTS

Universally known as "Allen" bolts, (Allen is a trade name) these Socket Headed Cap Screws are the preferred fastener for many bikers. The small head can be an advantage in many situations and these fasteners are reputed to be extremely durable, but most people use them for their apparent precision and that intangible feel of quality they lend to anything they touch.

Like all the other hardware you buy, you now have to be careful where, and from whom, you buy your SHCS bolts. In particular, the chrome plated variety are often only about a Grade 5, but you don't know unless you ask. The other problem that comes along with these nifty fasteners is the relatively long threads, which may have to be

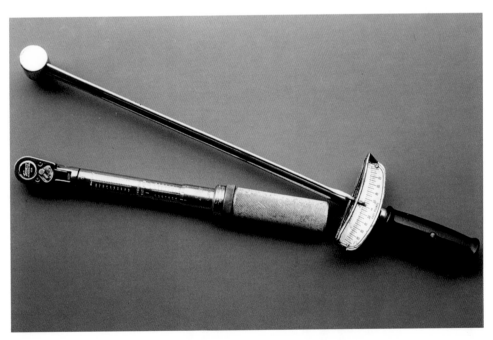

What keeps a bolt tight (besides Loctite) is tension. A properly tightened bolt actually stretches slightly like a spring, keeping tension on the threads. The only way to know how tight is tight is with a torque wrench. Use factory specifications whenever possible.

Any major motorcycle building project requires tools, and though they might seem extravagant, a set of dies (above) and taps (below) is really essential...

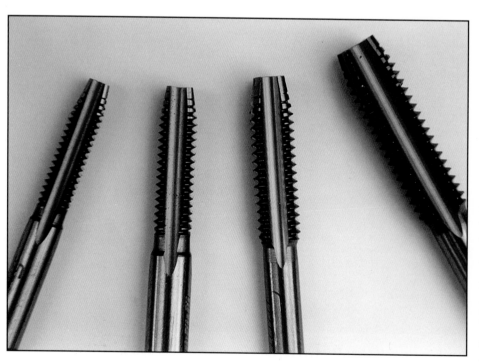

...when the frame comes back from the painter, you need to chase all the threads. When that one bolt won't screw in easily, you have to clean the threads in the hole. If Snap-on is too rich for your blood, stop down to the local Sears store.

shortened with a die-grinder or hacksaw. The small size means it's hard to use the full strength of the bolt to clamp things together. And if you use a standard stamped washer under the head it will deform later leaving you with a loose bolt. The answer is to use a hardened and ground washer under the head of the SHCS bolt.

The only thing better than an SHCS is one with a button head. These little rounded heads look like rivets. The button head however, allows for only a very shallow female socket, meaning you can't get a good grip with the wrench. So don't use the button heads when you need serious clamping pressure.

CHROME BOLTS

There are a couple of problems with chrome bolts. First, chrome plating a bolt weakens it slightly. Compensation may be provided if the manufacturer started with a high quality bolt. The other problem is the fact that these bolts have no markings on the head, so there is no easy way to judge their quality. Thus it's extra important that you purchase the bolts from a supplier you trust to provide good quality fasteners. If in doubt about any bolt or nut (especially chrome ones), it's a good idea to chase the threads with a tap or die. If the die or tap is doing much cutting, there's a problem and the best approach is to look for a replacement.

The use of chrome plated SHCS can be filled with frustration. Anyone who has used these bolts soon discovers that rust often develops down inside the head, due to the fact that the chrome plating process just can't get plating down into those crevices. The answer is to use the little chrome caps that snap into the socket, paint the inside of the heads, or put a dab of clear silicon on the end of the wrench the first time the bolt is used.

Because the chrome can flake off the fastener, even a good one, and cause it to bind in the hole, a good anti seize should be used on chrome bolts. Loctite products also do a good job of preventing metal to metal contact and can also be used to prevent galling of chrome nuts and bolts. Most of these bolts are Grade 5 or Grade 8, which means you want to be sure they don't gall and break off in the hole. Because they're so tough, they're also hard as hell to drill out and extract.

STAINLESS FASTENERS

Another way to get a shiny bolt or nut is to use stainless hardware. And while it is pretty and won't discolor, it simply isn't as strong as most good steel bolts. In fact, a Grade 8 stainless bolt is only about as good as a Grade 2 or 3 SAE steel bolt. The additional problem is the tendency of stainless to gall when the same bright material is used for both the nut and bolt. This ability to readily gall means you need to use anti-seize, or Loctite, on the threads of any stainless fasteners to prevent metal to metal contact.

Inch Torque Approximations for Non-Critical Applications Only
Atlantic™ Fasteners

SAE GRADE 5
Coarse Thread

SIZE	CLAMP LOAD	PLAIN	PLATED
1/4 - 20 (.250)	2,025	8 ft. lbs.	76 in. lbs.
5/16 - 18 (.3125)	3,338	17 ft. lbs.	13 ft. lbs.
3/8 - 16 (.375)	4,950	31 ft. lbs.	23 ft. lbs.
7/16 - 14 (.4375)	6,788	50 ft. lbs.	37 ft. lbs.
1/2 - 13 (.500)	9,075	76 ft. lbs.	57 ft. lbs.
9/16 - 12 (.5625)	11,625	109 ft. lbs.	82 ft. lbs.
5/8 - 11 (.625)	14,400	150 ft. lbs.	112 ft. lbs.
3/4 - 10 (.750)	21,300	266 ft. lbs.	200 ft. lbs.
7/8 - 9 (.875)	29,475	430 ft. lbs.	322 ft. lbs.
1 - 8 (1.000)	38,625	644 ft. lbs.	483 ft. lbs.
1-1/8 - 7 (1.125)	42,375	794 ft. lbs.	596 ft. lbs.
1-1/4 - 7 (1.250)	53,775	1120 ft. lbs.	840 ft. lbs.
1-3/8 - 6 (1.375)	64,125	1470 ft. lbs.	1102 ft. lbs.
1-1/2 - 6 (1.500)	78,000	1950 ft. lbs.	1462 ft. lbs.

SAE GRADE 5
Fine Thread

SIZE	CLAMP LOAD	PLAIN	PLATED
1/4 - 28 (.250)	2,325	10 ft. lbs.	87 in. lbs.
5/16 - 24 (.3125)	3,675	19 ft. lbs.	14 ft. lbs.
3/8 - 24 (.375)	5,588	35 ft. lbs.	26 ft. lbs.
7/16 - 20 (.4375)	7,575	55 ft. lbs.	41 ft. lbs.
1/2 - 20 (.500)	10,200	85 ft. lbs.	64 ft. lbs.
9/16 - 18 (.5625)	12,975	122 ft. lbs.	91 ft. lbs.
5/8 - 18 (.625)	16,350	170 ft. lbs.	128 ft. lbs.
3/4 - 16 (.750)	23,775	297 ft. lbs.	223 ft. lbs.
7/8 - 14 (.875)	32,475	474 ft. lbs.	355 ft. lbs.
1 - 12 (1.000)	42,300	705 ft. lbs.	529 ft. lbs.
1-14 (1.000)	32,275	721 ft. lbs.	541 ft. lbs.
1-1/8-12 (1.125)	47,475	890 ft. lbs.	668 ft. lbs.
1-1/4-12 (1.250)	59,550	1241 ft. lbs.	930 ft. lbs.
1-3/8-12 (1.375)	72,975	1672 ft. lbs.	1254 ft. lbs.
1-1/2-12 (1.500)	87,750	2194 ft. lbs.	1645 ft. lbs.

SAE GRADE 8
Coarse Thread

SIZE	CLAMP LOAD	PLAIN	PLATED
1/4 - 20 (.250)	2,850	12 ft. lbs.	9 ft. lbs.
5/16 - 18 (.3125)	4,725	25 ft. lbs.	18 ft. lbs.
3/8 - 16 (.375)	6,975	44 ft. lbs.	33 ft. lbs.
7/16 - 14 (.4375)	9,600	70 ft. lbs.	52 ft. lbs.
1/2 - 13 (.500)	12,750	106 ft. lbs.	80 ft. lbs.
9/16 - 12 (.5625)	16,350	153 ft. lbs.	115 ft. lbs.
5/8 - 11 (.625)	20,325	212 ft. lbs.	159 ft. lbs.
3/4 - 10 (.750)	30,075	376 ft. lbs.	282 ft. lbs.
7/8 - 9 (.875)	41,550	606 ft. lbs.	454 ft. lbs.
1 - 8 (1.000)	54,525	909 ft. lbs.	682 ft. lbs.
1-1/8 - 7 (1.125)	68,700	1288 ft. lbs.	966 ft. lbs.
1-1/4 - 7 (1.250)	87,225	1817 ft. lbs.	1363 ft. lbs.
1-3/8 - 6 (1.375)	103,950	2382 ft. lbs.	1787 ft. lbs.
1-1/2 - 6 (1.500)	126,450	3161 ft. lbs.	2371 ft. lbs.

SAE GRADE 8
Fine Thread

SIZE	CLAMP LOAD	PLAIN	PLATED
1/4 - 28 (.250)	3,263	14 ft. lbs.	10 ft. lbs.
5/16 - 24 (.3125)	5,113	27 ft. lbs.	20 ft. lbs.
3/8 - 24 (.375)	7,875	49 ft. lbs.	37 ft. lbs.
7/16 - 20 (.4375)	10,650	78 ft. lbs.	58 ft. lbs.
1/2 - 20 (.500)	14,400	120 ft. lbs.	90 ft. lbs.
9/16 - 18 (.5625)	18,300	172 ft. lbs.	129 ft. lbs.
5/8 - 18 (.625)	23,025	240 ft. lbs.	180 ft. lbs.
3/4 - 16 (.750)	33,600	420 ft. lbs.	315 ft. lbs.
7/8 - 14 (.875)	45,825	668 ft. lbs.	501 ft. lbs.
1 - 12 (1.000)	59,700	995 ft. lbs.	746 ft. lbs.
1-14 (1.000)	61,125	1019 ft. lbs.	764 ft. lbs.
1-1/8-12 (1.125)	77,025	1444 ft. lbs.	1083 ft. lbs.
1-1/4-12 (1.250)	96,600	2012 ft. lbs.	1509 ft. lbs.
1-3/8-12 (1.375)	118,350	2712 ft. lbs.	2034 ft. lbs.
1-1/2-12 (1.500)	142,275	3557 ft. lbs.	2668 ft. lbs.

Ideally, you should use the torque specifications from the factory service manual. But when no other specifications are available, these guidelines from Atlantic Fasteners will help.

Chapter Six

Metric Choppers

Part 1 - Kawachoppa

THE ULTIMATE CHEAP CHOPPER

When it comes to building a cheap chopper, metric rides are about as cheap as they come. Which doesn't make them bad by any means. The two most common powerplants, the

900/1000 Kawasaki and the single cam 750 Honda, are very durable and (at least in the case of the Kawasaki) fairly powerful engines. Better yet, thousands and thousands were manufactured and sold in the US, and a fair percentage of these

Some bikes are more scratch-built than others. This one from Steve Tersteeg uses a Kawasaki 1000 engine set in his own fabricated frame. Not as cheap as it might have been, one of Steve's goals was to give the bike a nice "modern vibe."

bikes are currently available at garage sale prices. Presented in this chapter are two projects, one Kawasaki and one Honda. The first metric chopper, a Kawasaki, is the work of Steve Tersteeg of Savage, Minnesota. These are the photos that illustrate Part I of this chapter. Steve not only built his own frame and assembled his own motorcycle, he took his own photos and wrote the accompanying text as well. As Steve mentions in his story that follows, "building a frame from scratch is not for everybody." And finding hardtail frames with mounts for Kawasaki engines isn't the easiest thing either. There's a spot on the web called Mike's Choppers (see Sources) but otherwise most Metric hardtail frames are designed for the 750 Honda. Many frame manufacturers however, will install mounts for a Kawasaki in a frame normally meant for a Honda mill (for more on metric frames read the interview with Ken Kuhnke in Part II of this chapter).

Building a metric ride is generally more challenging because there aren't the huge catalogs full of every available part and adapter that there are on the V-twin side of the market. Much of what's out there is old stock and

The start of the The Kawachoppa building sequence by Steve Tersteeg: This is one of the first times the "roller" came down from the table. I really wanted to see how it felt on the ground. Three-and-a-half inches of ground clearance seems to be about the minimum for anything that's going to see street duty.

The inline four-cylinder fits with room to spare. At this point, one set of front mounts is tacked into place. Note the fiberglass seat pan, which was formed in place on the frame. It ensures a snug fit when done this way.

Another view of the "roller". Buddy, the shop dog, has been following the project closely and occasionally has suggestions.

old stuff from the 1970s. Ebay, the web in general, and the local swap meet in particular, are good places to look for parts. Which is not to say you should ignore the huge aftermarket catalogs from Drag Specialties, Custom Chrome and all the rest. Parts are parts whether the engine uses two cylinders or four.

As Ken Kuhnke implies in his interview, the people building Metric choppers are often very price conscious. Which is fine, except when the search for the least expensive engine, fender or frame becomes an obsession and any sense of value is lost.

The problem of being too cheap is two-fold. First, cheap stuff often doesn't work and fit as well. Now you, or someone you hire, needs to modify the frame so the engine fits, or mud up the fender because it's in such rough shape. You've lost both time and money. Second, and more important, cheap stuff may not be as safe. You're going to ride this machine, often with a significant other on the back. You need good brakes, good tires, and predictable handling. When you buy a two-hundred dollar frame with a neck that isn't true, or a five dollar

The gas tank and rear fender have been added to the mock-up. The Fat Katz rear fender blank has been marked for trimming. The inner radius matches that of the PMFR rim's outside edge. The tank really worked out well in the seat transition area. Only minor sheet metal was added to make things match up nicely.

Back on the table for more surgery. The next task was to trim and mount the rear fender.

Mounting bosses have been added in 4 places to secure the rear fender. Lower ones ultimately didn't work and had to be changed for chain clearance.

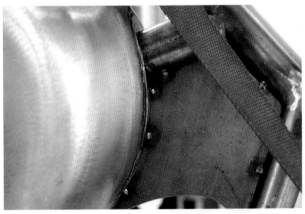

Neck gussets were mocked up out of tag board, transferred to .125 mild steel, and tacked into place. I paid special attention to the curve at the bottom in order for it to flow into the lines of the tank.

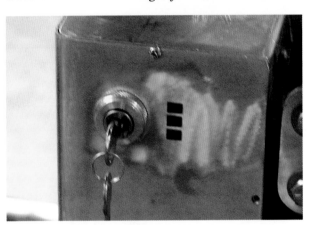

A close-up reveals the marine ignition switch (brass, very reliable) and the LED indicators for ignition, oil pressure, and high beam. Not easy to see when riding, but better than none.

As noted in the text, the aluminum battery box contains all the bike's electrical components.

Close-up of the rear axle adjusters and HHI rigid-mount rear caliper. The Russell rotors have subsequently been changed to matching PMFR Bonesters.

The rear fender is trimmed and mounted. The tail-light wiring is routed through the frame from the battery box. It passes through a hollow bolt in the lower mount and into the fender's wiring tube.

caliper that's been in the guy's damp garage for ten years, you compromise function and safety. Think about what it is you're trying to achieve and keep that goal in mind when deciding what to buy.

As many of these Japanese donor bikes are found in the back of garages and barns, it's important to note that tires don't always age well. Even when new, tires from 1980 weren't nearly as good as what we take for granted today. Add in wear and deterioration from sitting (especially if the bike or parts were outside part of the time) and you have a tire that's no longer safe to ride. If there's any doubt, spend a few bucks and put new rubber on the bike. Remember, if you have a flat or blowout on your car, there are three other tires and a lot of metal to keep your fanny up off the asphalt. If you lose a tire on a motorcycle, it's a whole 'nother story.

THE KAWACHOPPA BY STEVE TERSTEEG

I got interested in building an Asian-powered chopper after a friend acquired a sort-of "roller" rigged for a 750 Honda at a swap meet. I build V-twin customs for a living and there was something appealing about the economy and novelty of using Japanese

It's actually starting to look like something now. Still needs forward controls, exhaust, and the offset drive setup. The headlight pictured didn't look right. I knew that much more money would have to be thrown at this problem.

power. However, I didn't want to build a "retro" machine. It had to have current style, which included a wide rear tire, real brakes, modern sheet metal, and a decent front end. No 130-16 rear tire, mechanical drum brakes, coffin tank, or springer fork. The biggest constraint was the wide tire. Without it, there would be no project.

I found that Precision Metal Fab Racing (PMFR) in Shakopee, Minnesota, makes Suzuki and Kawasaki offset drive setups for drag bikes. With some modification, I was able to achieve the amount of offset necessary (2.3 inches) to use a 240-18 tire with the engine remaining centered in the chassis. Since there are virtually no new frames available, I chose to build one. A word of caution: This is not for everybody. It necessitates building a frame jig, buying a tubing bender, being able to create safe and cosmetically-appealing welds, and lots of patience. It also requires knowledge in the area of frame geometry, such as rake and trail measurements. A big help was having a noted expert to interrogate. As long as I was making things out of tubing I made the handlebars, too.

I was able to acquire a low-mileage 1982 Kawasaki CSR 1000 as a

Top front motor mounts in progress. The old rubber isolators were replaced with the aluminum pieces shown.

The rear motor mounts were fabricated from .250 inch 6061 aluminum stock. They were trimmed down and drilled for a sleeker appearance.

Front motor mount plates and frame bosses were added. They were also modified for appearance later.

The seat was upholstered in black Symphony simulated leather. Note the small filler panels added to the tail of the IGT tank and how the tank and seat fit together.

Concern about the peg-to-peg width of the forward controls on the inline-four engine lead to a comparison with a V-twin bike. They only ended up being about 3 inches wider. Not a problem.

A view from the back is starting to show that, stylistically, something's missing behind the seat.

Right-side brake pedal/master cylinder. Braided line is routed through the lower frame tubing to rear caliper. Banjo-bolt brake switch is used to eliminate the extra pressure switch, block and extra fittings.

The stock transmission cover will be replaced with a modified PMFR cover. An offset sprocket will be added to compensate for the width of the 240-18 Metzeler rear tire.

donor bike. I removed the engine/transmission and some of the electrical components and sold the rest to recoup half of my four hundred dollar investment.

Now that's an inexpensive driveline. Lots of cereal boxes were sacrificed in the name of developing the mounting bosses and brackets necessary to attach the engine to the frame. The great part is that once the engine is mounted all you need to add is gasoline, electricity, and a chain and you're underway: There is no separate tranny, primary, or oil tank to mess with. Sound simple? Trust me, it's not. There's a lot of machining and fabrication work involved when you're making all "one-off" parts.

Lots of hours went into modifying and fitting the fender blanks I used. The rear fender placement on a rigid is extremely critical to the look of the bike. That, along with figuring out where to put the license/taillight and adding internal struts, consumed what seemed to be enormous amounts of time.

A license plate pan was formed out of 16 gauge mild steel and TIG welded into the rear fender. Nuts were welded in place for plate attachment, as there's virtually no room to get your fin-

This Headwinds headlight was what I was looking for (sans the shrink-wrap). Much better!

The exhaust system was fabricated out of 1.5" mild steel tubing, using various bends and straights to achieve the fit shown. A certain amount of luck prevailed relative to working around the confines of the forward controls.

The rear fender with final trim. Taillight and license plate are still lacking. I'm not a fan of sidemounts on wide tire bikes, so something else was in order.

A side view of the cleaned-up motor showing the right side exhaust routing.

The 4-into-4 exhaust had baffles installed in the straight sections prior to welding on the turnouts.

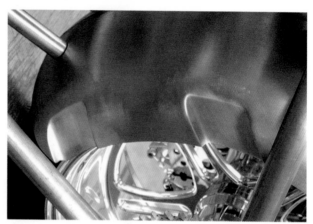

Rather than cut an ugly gash in the side of the fender for chain clearance, I opted for these hand-formed recesses. That way the inner radius of the fender is preserved when looking at it from the left side.

A left side view of the exhaust routing and clearance issues around the shift control.

A license plate pan and taillight mount were formed by hand and then welded into the fender blank.

gers in there to do anything. A bezel and LED assembly was pirated from a sidemount taillight. The contours that help it blend into the fender were mocked up in cardboard, transferred to metal, formed, and TIG welded into place using a silicon bronze rod, which requires much less heat and reduces distortion.

The Independent gas tank, while very expensive, only required some minor metalworking in the seat area. Speaking of the seat, the pan was molded from fiberglass after the frame was completed. I then sculpted the pad and sewed the cover out of simulated leather. Much nicer when it rains.

The wheels, brake rotors, and rear sprocket are Bonesters from PMFR. Brake calipers are HHI, hand controls are Joker Machine and the front end is a combination of Accutronix 5-degree trees and Midwest legs/sliders. The headlight is from Headwinds. These items cost a bundle, but remember I wanted a modern custom vibe. American Thunder in Prior Lake, Minnesota, sold me a set of used FXR forward controls that I modified to fit.

Once the bodywork, frame molding, and Galaxy Silver

The completed rear fender. Although not visible in the picture, .125" internal struts were TIG-welded into the inner radii of the fender to stiffen it. Therefore, no typical rigid fender struts were necessary.

Swoopy gussets were added to smooth the transition from the seat to the rear fender, maintaining the flow from the neck to the tail of the bike.

Ready for disassembly. Anything that doesn't fit now (and some things that do) will definitely not fit after paint.

basecoat/clearcoat paint-work was done, final assembly began. I should mention that it's very important to make sure everything fits together before doing any of this. The entire bike was "dry built", right down to the chain, before being disassembled for finishing. Only the wiring was left until after. Speaking of wiring, I put all the bike's electrical components, including battery, regulator/rectifier, ignition module, headlight relay, solenoid, and circuit breakers in the aluminum battery box. The heat-producing components (regulator/rectifier and ignition module) are mounted on the front vertical surface where they can receive some all-important air flow.

This project, while neither very cheap or real expensive, proved to be a great opportunity in many ways. First, it was way easier to be creative when I was working on my own design with parts I made. I've always found it much more difficult to hack up and modify things that I've already paid a lot of money for. Second, I have a much greater appreciation for chassis builders. And, finally, there's a great sense of satisfaction in doing something a little bit different.

The carbs had to be rejetted to compensate for the "shorty" air filters and the low-restriction exhaust. Adapting the H-D type throttle cable to the Mikunis required machining a small adapter. Stock Kawasaki coils are hidden up in the tank's tunnel.

The end result.

Complete at last!

Chapter Six

Metric Choppers

Part 2 - Honda Chop

The most popular of the Metric choppers are the bikes based on a 750 Honda drivetrain. Though the Kawasaki engines have more power, when it comes to assembling a chopper the Honda is by far the more popular donor bike.

Anyone building a Honda chopper benefits because parts, from frames to exhaust systems, are easier to find.

The relative popularity of the two bikes is about the same now as it was during the first

For this project Tom Summers started with an old Smith Bros and Fetrow hardtail Honda frame from the 1970s.

phaze of chopper building in the 1970s. Thus many of the parts that people are using to build current Honda choppers were manufactured thirty years ago. The current wave of popularity for choppers means though that many new companies are once again providing new parts for your project. Besides the web, check out some of the new magazines like Chopper Underground.

One of the men who's been through it all, from the the late 1960s to the current resurgent wave of chopper building is Tom Summers of Lowriders by Summers in Minneapolis. The mock-up 750 chopper seen here is one of Tom's projects, unfinished as we go to press unfortunately. None the less, the project is fairly representative of the very functional bike you can build from readily available parts.

Many of the parts Tom used for this project are in fact used. Including the hardtail frame and the four-into-two exhaust (Tom is a frequent buyer on Ebay). The photos illustrate the parts Tom used and why, along with some of the ways in which Tom overcomes little problems you're likely to encounter as you put together your first 750 Honda chopper.

By way of contrast, this is a new hardtail frame, designed for the 750 Honda engine, that Tom sells.

Like most Honda chopper builders, Tom used a rear wheel assembly made up of the original hub mated to a 40 spoke chrome aftermarket rim.

53

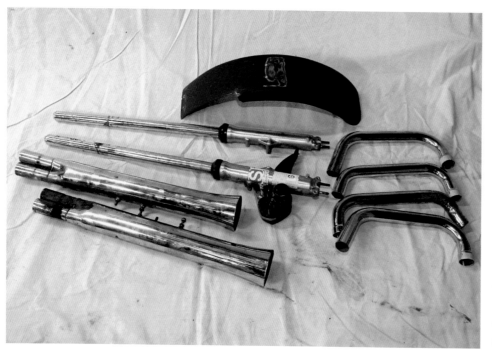

Both the exhaust and the tube assemblies (with 8 inch over tubes) were purchased used. The exhaust is still usable and will be sent out for plating.

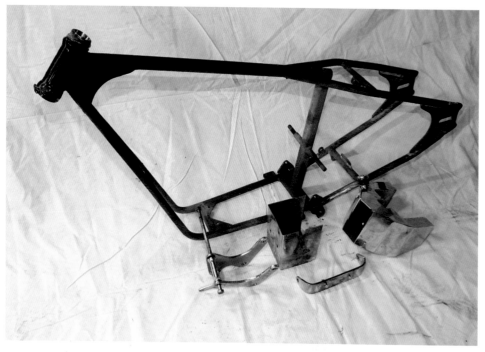

The used frame is in good condition and shows no evidence of any accidents. With a little molding and fresh paint the old chassis will be as good as new.

INTERVIEW, KEN KUHNKE

For a little additional insight into the process of building a Honda 750 chopper, we had a conversation with Ken Kuhnke, owner of Cycle Exchange in Minoqua, Wisconsin, Ken manufactures everything from frames to two-carb intake set ups for Honda choppers. Kenny is one of those quiet men, with a lot to say - you just have to listen.

Ken, tell us about frames, how hard is it to find a hardtail frame for a Honda and what should a person look for in a frame or a frame manufacturer?

People are coming out of woodwork building frames, you may not want to buy from them. Be very careful what you buy. Find someone with experience. A reputable company that's been in business for awhile. Our frames, and all good frames, are made from DOM tubing (drawn over mandrel). And all the welding should be done with a tig welder.

If the frames are really cheap ask yourself why. Some are so bad the axles aren't even level to the ground and the rake is way off. Use some common sense.

What about a Kawasaki, does anyone make frames for a Kawasaki?

All the companies I know of are making Honda frames, so a Kawi frame is a special order, that's how we do it.

Back to Hondas. Which exhaust systems do you recommend and why?

Honda choppers have what I call ground clearance issues. You should have six inches of clearance, that isn't too bad. It's hard to find good pipes for the Hondas. Most people run Mac drag pipes, those are pretty high up. But drag pipes don't make a lot of power and they're hard to tune. A 4 into 1 is a better design, the engines like those systems, but most of them go under the bike so you loose ground clearance.

What about wiring and electronics. What do you use for a harness?

No one makes a harness, you have to build your own, there are wring diagrams on the web. It's fairly simple, you only have a couple of wires if there aren't any blinkers. We have kits with solid state rectifiers, the stock ones are butt ugly and they don't work. We also have chrome coils. Stock coils are ugly and the wires are permanently fixed in

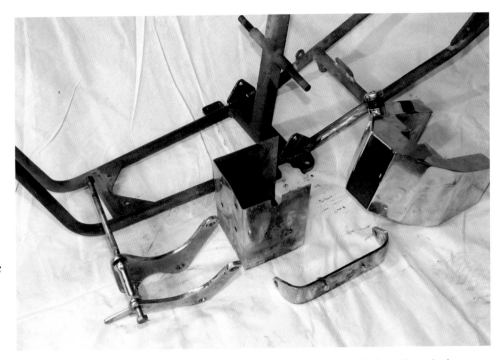

The frame came complete with the oil tank, battery box and engine mounting plates.

After taking the mock-up bike apart, this is the group of parts that are going out for fresh plating.

55

The rear tire is a 130X16 inch, while up front Tom used a 19 inch Avon. (Always use caution before using used rubber).

The pipes seen here are a good find, "because the engine runs better than it does with straight pipes, and they run along side the frame which doesn't hurt the ground clearance."

place. We run different coils and use our own wires, they look better and offer more flexibility in the placement.

How wide a back tire can you run with the Honda motor, assuming the engine is in the center of the frame?

We take the stock rear hub, combine that with a 40-spoke four-inch rim meant for a Harley-Davidson and mount a 160 tire. We make the rear fender shorter because the shorter fender makes the rear tire look wider.

What are some of the other parts, besides the engine and rear hub, that can be used?

The stock Honda front end works pretty well, you can get new, longer, tubes from Forking by Frank's. And the bars and controls can be used again.

What are the mistakes people make when they build a Honda Chopper, especially for the first time?

They spend their money on the wrong things. People spend too much on cosmetics and don't worry about things like the quality of the frame. They don't always have basic mechanical skills, some of them don't even own tools. They watch cable TV and think that's pretty cool so they want to do it themselves. Yet, there are certain skills you need to build these bikes. They start with a hardtail frame that's pretty raw, now you need spacers for the axles. Those have to be cut on a lathe. And the tabs usually aren't welded on to mount the oil tank and gas tank, that requires welding skills. These bikes are probably harder to build than people think. It's nice to have some skilled people around you when you start one of these projects, people who've been dealing with motorcycles for awhile and have some of the necessary skills.

Creativity in action. The tank is a peanut tank that Tom cut in half. Once he decided whether or not he likes the look of the stretched version, it will go back to the fabricator for final welding, then out for paint.

As evidenced in the Redneck/Buell chapter, an old nasty looking engine can be made to look fresh and clean with just a little elbow grease and paint.

Chapter Seven

Frank's Digger

A Simple Hardtail Built In-House

Choppers come in all shapes and sizes, with all types of powerplants. The assembly seen here is done at Frank Pedersen's Motorcycle Works in Olathe, Kansas.

Inspired by chopper builders in his native Norway, Frank started building choppers well before this current Chopper Craze Phaze Two began. About the time he started building choppers, Frank also started fabricating and selling what he calls his Street Fighter frames. Available in big twin or Sportster configura-

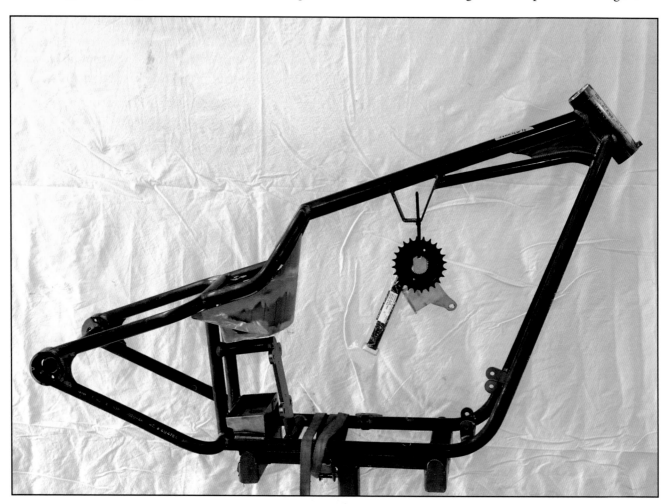

This is the frame as sold, with oil tank, offset sprocket (this is a 240 tire frame), rear axle, battery box welded in, battery strap, 4 quart oil tank, oil filler cap, and top motor mount. The frame also includes a welded on kick stand tab and welded on fork stops.

tions, these hardtail, low neck frames caught on quickly as a foundation for simple back-to-basics high performance motorcycles. Of the two configurations though, the Sportster/Buell frames easily out sold their bigger, supposedly faster, brothers.

As we go to press, the tall raised neck choppers are all the rage. Though Frank has built his fair share of those super long, super tall bikes he wanted to try something new. Call it a hybrid. A perfect melding of the low neck street fighter frame with the tall stretched chopper frames.

Seen here is the mock-up assembly of Frank's new Digger frame. A frame with 40 degrees of rake and a neck positioned two inches up and two inches out. At the front Frank chose a hydraulic 41mm fork, made up of six-over softail custom tubes, located in seven-degree trees. By Frank's calculation the combination of 40 degree neck and seven degree trees gives exactly 3-3/4 inches of trail, a figure that will yield a good handling motorcycle.

MOCK-UP, STAGE ONE

The mock-up was actually done in two stages. Before the frame was completely finished Frank and crew install a mock up motor, front end and rear wheel - just to see how everything lines up and fits in the new frame design. Then it all has to come apart again for final welding of the rear "fender" and some additional brackets before coming back into the main shop for the "final" mock-up. If it sound confusing, it isn't. Just follow along as Frank shows us how to assemble a hardtail chopper with a Sportster (or Buell) drivetrain. Obviously when you build a Sportster-based chopper or digger there will only be (hopefully) one mock up session and one final assembly.

The frames are welded up in-house in jigs of Frank's manufacture from heavy wall mild steel. "I use only DOM (drawn over mandrel, a high quality tubing designation) mild steel tubing," explains Frank. "The backbone is 1-5/8 inch tubing with .188 inch walls while the rest of the frame is 1-1/4 inch with 120 inch wall thickness." All the welds are done with heli-arc equipment and because Frank likes to keep everything in-house, even the bends are done on equipment in the frame room.

Frank has these trees make to his specifications, seven degrees in this case.

Adjusting the trees is a matter of achieving minimal pre-load and zero end play.

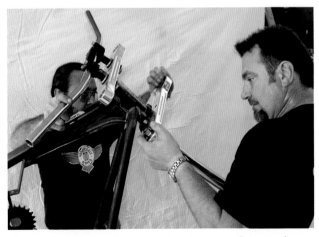

Once the trees are in place the 41mm tubes can be slipped into place.

There's a rubber seal and a chrome washer under the head of each top cap.

Here you can see the right side spacers and the axle (before the cap on the lower leg is tightened).

The innermost wheel spacer used on either side slips past the seal and butts up against the outside of the inner bearing race.

The rear brake is a swap-meet special with a long cast tab that anchors the caliper on a stock frame.

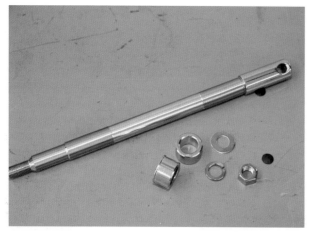

The axle kit comes with spacers, but probably not the ones you need to center the wheel between the legs.

The solution is to knock off the tab and neatly grind the area to match the other end of the caliper. Matching black paint will be next.

TRIPLE TREES

The front triple trees are wide glide (which refers to the spacing of the fork legs) style, manufactured to Frank's specifications. These will add seven degrees of rake to the fork tubes (see Chapter Three for more on rake and trail). Frank and Daniel work together to install the trees. Once the bearings are properly adjusted the 41mm tubes can be slid up into place and locked there with the top fork nut and seal.

INSTALL FRONT WHEEL

The 21 inch front wheel is from DNA, laced up so the hub is in the center of the wheel. As Frank explains, "We set the wheel up in the middle of the tubes, but the factory puts the wheel in with some offset." Frank and Daniel (the mechanic responsible for much of the assembly) use a FXST axle and spacer kit to install the wheel. This front wheel uses a 3/4 inch axle with tapered bearings. See Chapter Ten For more on setting up the end play when using tapered wheel bearings. There aren't enough spacers in the axle kit to center the wheel so Frank uses some pre-cut aluminum spacers that he keeps in stock.

INSTALL REAR WHEEL

The rear wheel is another DNA item, laced per Frank's instructions so the right side chain sprocket will line up with the offset transmission sprocket. "I'm going to try to use a swap-meet Dyna rear caliper here," says Frank, "along with the standard axle kit. But in order to use this caliper we have to cut off the long extension that locks it to the tab on a stock frame. This is the kind of thing you have to do if you're going to build an inexpensive motorcycle." The rear wheel uses a one-inch axle and sealed bearings, which means the rear brake rotor needs to be year -2000 and up. Otherwise you have to enlarge the center hole to fit the enlarged hub used with a 1 inch axle.

Frank advises builder to, "Spend the money where it counts, get the frame and the motorcycle you want, if you want a fat tire buy the frame and wheels you want, skimp on things like controls and accessories, you can always change those parts out later."

It's a good idea to clean out all the threads on the frame and the hubs with a tap before any bolts are screwed in.

A test fit with a different rotor shows the need for a inner spacer between the wheel bearing and the caliper bracket.

Here Daniel and Frank set the mock-up engine in place.

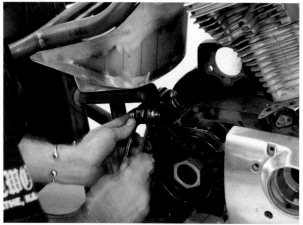

Four bolts mount the rear of the engine/transmission to the plate at the back of the frame.

Just for reference, here's a shot of a stock late-model Sportster with factory forward controls.

Stock Sportster engine mounting plates are used up front.

To check rear wheel and drivetrain alignment Frank first checks that the wheel is centered, using the two lower frame rails as reference points.

These particular plates have a big hole in the center for (Sportster) highway pegs.

Then a piece of square stock is clamped to the transmission sprocket to check alignment of the two sprockets.

At this point the boys install the designated mock up engine. "On most of our bikes we use forward controls for a Sportster Custom," explains Frank. "Those are H-D #33891-98 and come with the front engine mounting plates. On this bike we decided to go with big twin forward controls. "With our frames we've tried to make it really easy to just drop the engine and transmission right in. The tabs are in the same location as they are on factory bikes."

When asked, Frank reports that, "Sporty and Buell cases are the same, but Buells use larger bolts at the rear motor mount plate. When someone tells us they are buying the frame for a Buell motor we drill out the holes for the rear mounting plate."

DRIVELINE ALIGNMENT

Using tubing or conduit and the two main lower frame tubes for reference, Frank checks that the rear wheel is parallel to the tubes and centered in the frame. Next he clamps a piece of square tubing to the transmission sprocket, to check the position of the rear sprocket. The two sprockets should line up of course, in some cases you might have to use an offset rear sprocket or a spacer between the hub and the sprocket.

GAS TANK

To give the bike a chopper profile Frank sets one of his chopper gas tanks on the top tube. To determine the position of the tank, it's necessary to check that nothing hits the tank when the forks are turned. Once Frank determines where the tank should sit the top tube is marked for later.

A FEW WORDS ON PIPES

We are using big twin forward controls on this bike and the stock-type pipes will hit those controls. The answer to this dilemma is to make a set of pipes, it's not as hard as it sounds. "A lot of this depends on what you have for a donor bike," explains Frank. "Whether you start with a Buell or a Sportster and whether or not the Sportster has forward controls."

"We make our exhausts up from Softail Custom pipes that we buy cheap at the swap meets. Just cut them up and then weld them back together. When I do stepped pipes, I hammer the

With a caliper and calculator Frank determines how thick an axle spacer is needed on each side of the rear wheel hub.

A simple strap of 3/16 steel and a small tab (that will be final-welded later) are used to locate the rear wheel caliper.

Attachment of the short header pipe is how the job of fabricating pipes begins.

Another piece is added to the short exhaust stub.

Fabricating pipes requires equal measures of available bends (and pipe sections) and patience.

The big U-shaped bends are bent up by an outside vendor, then sections can be cut out as needed to fabricate an exhaust system like this one.

By working the edge of the stepped up pipe Frank is able to reduce the diameter so it's a better fit, and thicken the metal so it's easier to weld.

The rear exhaust pipe is pieced together in much the same way as the front.

The final welds are done with a tig-welder, though for the mock-up a wire-feed welder works very well.

edge of the bigger pipe so it fits the smaller pipe better, this also thickens the metal at the edge, or collects it, so it's easier to weld without burning through. I use a small wire-feed welder to tack these together then we do the final welds with tig and finish them with jet coat or ceramic coating."

"I put a 3/8 inch pin across the exhaust near the exit on the rear pipe (check the photos), on the front pipe I put it farther up in the pipe. Both pins are about the same distance from the exhaust valve. What we're actually trying to do is provide each cylinder with the same volume between the exhaust valve and the restriction. The pins actually do two things: They make the engine see two pipes that are the same length, and they provide enough back pressure that the engine runs better in the midrange than it does with straight pipes – without hurting the top end power."
(copy continues on page 71)

INTERVIEW, FRANK PEDERSEN FROM MOTORCYCLE WORKS.

Frank, can we start with a little background on you and how you became involved with motorcycles?

When I moved here in 1984 I started as an aircraft mechanic apprentice, then started painting airplanes, small ones. Eventually I got back into cars, restoration and repair, making panels that you couldn't buy, that kind of thing. That's what I did in Norway.

From restoration and repair I ended up with a used car lot and I didn't like that. So in 1993 or early 1994 I started messing with motorcycles in my garage at home. Then in March of 1995 I opened up Motorcycle Works. To start with we did service and repairs on just about anything.

About that time I built a bike, a '74 Sporty motor in a Paugcho frame. Next I bought a wrecked '79 FLH and a Santee frame and built a custom bike out of that.

In summer of 1995 I went to Norway on vacation, I visited Chopper Freaks, a club in my hometown in Norway. They were building long, low bikes, choppers without the raised neck. When I came home I built one of those, it was one of the first bikes to be built with a 200X16

The finished pipes prior to final welding and some kind of coating.

Here you can see one of the two 3/8 inch pins described in the text. The one in the forward pipe is located farther up the pipe as explained in the text.

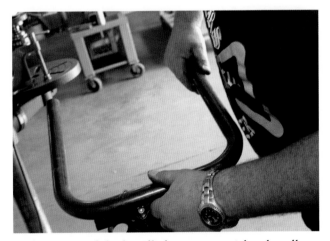
Fabrication of the handle bars starts with a handle bar clamp, one piece of straight one-inch tubing and another piece of larger diameter frame tubing.

Making the bars requires many cuts and tack welds.

Now Mike welds up that part of the assembly before...

The big cutoff wheel is used to cut the radius out of the larger diameter tubing.

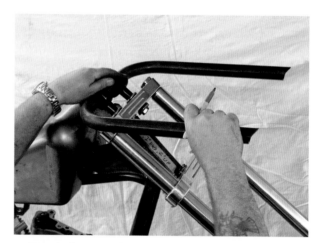

...Frank does another test fit. Then the bars are cut shorter...

A test fit shows that Frank is moving in the right direction.

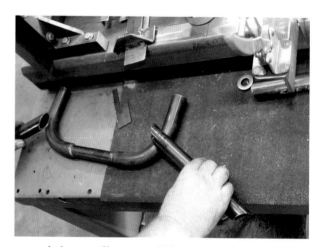

...and the cutoff piece will be used to form part of the junction where the bars turn back.

inch rear tire. That was a long bike with 47 degree rake, built on a Chopper Guys frame.

In the spring of 1996 I went to the show in Cincinnati and showed pictures of the bike to everybody there. They all said 'why did you build a chopper?' I said, 'because they're coming back.' They all thought I was nuts, the only one doing choppers then was Pat Kennedy.

In 1996 we built our first frame, we designed it for a Sportster engine. That winter we built the first street fighter, designed for a '73 Sporty motor. It was our own frame with a drop seat. In July of '96 we went to a bigger shop, 1500 sq. ft. In 1999 we built a hardtail frame that used a solid-mounted twin cam Dyna engine. By this time people are starting to talk about choppers and diggers, digger is more of a drag race style bike, uses a lower neck and lots of rake.

You were one of the first of the current builders to use Sportster/Buell drivetrains as the basis for your choppers, why do you like the Sportster/Buell motor so much?

Cost is the simple answer. A lot of people have a Sportster or Sportster engine and want a cool bike so I started building frames for them. When we built that bike in 2000 based on a Buell we discovered what a great donor bike a Buell is. Last year 75% of our frames were Sporty frames, but now we're starting to get calls for big twin engines.

You sell frames, rolling chassis kits and complete bikes?

Almost half of the chopper frames go out of here as rolling chassis kits, with seat pan, the fenders and gas tank mounted. It makes things simpler for the customer. The rake and trail are correct, any brackets are tig welded on in the right place, everything fits. We've figured out how long the fork tubes should be. When you're done you don't end up with a pile of parts you can't use.

If I buy a chassis kit from you, approximately how much will the entire project cost?

You can build a Sportster chopper for less than ten thousand dollars. You could also spend twice that depending on the parts. We have one customer who spent over 30K on a street fighter,

More cutting, a little tack welding and...

...Frank is ready for a test ride on the hoist.

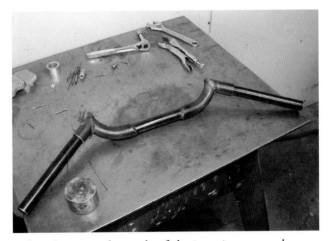

After changing the angle of the junction once, the bars are deemed both stylish and comfortable. All that's left is final welding.

The controls were scrounged at a swap meet.

Frames can be ordered with or without big-twin-style forward controls.

Now Frank and Daniel mount the controls (minus the ball-ends) to the bars.

At this point the rear "fender" framework is in place.

The frame goes back in the shop for attachment of the forward control mounts and a few additional brackets.

Next comes fabrication of the sheet metal insert, which starts with a paper pattern...

but that included a big bore kit on the Buell motor that we bought. We didn't use a donor bike we just went out and bought the parts the customer wanted.

Using a donor bike is a cheaper way to go?

Yes, and a Buell is the most cost effective choice. The Buell has more horsepower than Sportster, better heads, cams and all the rest. To buy a donor of the same year/condition in a Sportster is generally more money and it isn't more motorcycle..

In terms of geometry, what is the range you like to see people stay within for rake, and then what kind of trail figures do you like to stay within?

With our bikes the center of gravity is very low so it's easier to maneuver, even for a first time rider. They feel light. I don't care much about the rake angle as long as trail is right. I keep them between 3-1/2 and 4 1/2 inches of trail, and I get that by using raked trees.

How hard is it to title a bike that's assembled from a new aftermarket frame and a donor-bike engine?

In Kansas you have to have a copy of the title for the bike that the engine came from, and a notarized bill of sale for that engine. And a manufacturers certificate of origin with receipt and notarized bill of sale for the frame. When we go to the DMV, we also have receipts for everything else, including the transmission if it's a big twin. In Kansas you have to take the finished bike to the highway patrol for an inspection, then take the paperwork they give you to a DMV station, with all the receipts, to get the title.

What do you prefer for frame material?

I don't like chrome moly because it work hardens and is prone to cracking, a thin wall chrome moly frame will transmit vibration, it won't absorb or dampen vibration like a thick-wall mild-steel frame will.

Aircraft use chrome moly, but they use big rubber mounts for the engine and the RPM is pretty low as well, compared to a motorcycle. I like DOM tubing, drawn over mandrel, it's what we use. This is the best material you can use to build a motorcycle frame. Aluminum doesn't

...which is used to cut out the sheet metal.

Once cut and shaped it can be welded to the tubing.

A piece of foam is used to keep the gas tank snug on the top tube while mounts are fabricated.

69

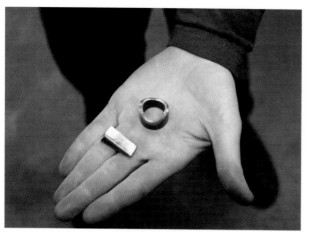
Small brackets are used between the tank mounting brackets and the bottom of the top tube.

The "finished" frame is back on the hoist, the 883 motor is in place and it's time to finish installing the rest of the controls and hydraulics.

Mike mounts the tank and the brackets in the position indicated by Frank...

The forward controls are pretty simple, blue Loctite should be used on the final assembly.

...before welding the brackets in place. One of the nice things about buying a rolling chassis kit is the fact that the tank brackets are correctly located and tig-welded in place.

Spacers located behind the drive sprocket. Early on right, later on left, with seals. Use later, thinner spacer and seal combination (about 5/8 inch thick) which allows use of a sprocket with thicker hub.

work, it cracks. We don't like aluminum gas tanks for that same reason.

What should buyers look for in a frame?

Ask the shops that build bikes which frames they like, do the parts fit? There are a few bad ones, a number of mediocre manufacturers and some very good ones.

Where do people make mistakes in assembling their own bike?

Most common mistake is to use a frame that's not right, they try to save money on the frame. If you are building a house and the foundation is crooked you are fighting it all the way through. But if the foundation is good then the whole job goes well. Buy a good frame and save the money someplace else. I like a frame that uses bigger diameter tubes and thicker walls because those tubes are better at absorbing vibration.

(copy continued from page 65)
Frank Builds Handle Bars Too

The handle bars are assembled with patience and many trial fits from various pieces of stock (note the photo sequence). The controls are swap-meet specials, devoid of the standard flange and without the ball on the end of the lever. After the bars are done they still touch the tank at full lock, "We'll have to add a little metal to the fork stop," says Frank.

Final Welding Sequence

Once the bars are complete the frame goes back into the frame department for the addition of big twin forward controls, the rear "fender" and a few brackets. Things like forward controls are part of the option list you have to fill out prior to purchase. All brackets and controls are in place when you buy one of Frank's frames.

The photos illustrate the various jigs and techniques used to install some of the components on the frame. The gas tanks that Frank uses come with four mounting bungs in the bottom. The fabricator's job is to set the tank on the top tube and then install the tank mounts to the bottom of the top tube.

The 530 chain from Tsubaki comes too long...

...and must be cut to the correct length. First the ends of the pins are ground off.

Then a chain breaker is used to push the pins out.

71

Then the master link and cover plate can be installed...

The aftermarket caliper is attached with bolts that came with the caliper. Brake line is attached with the aid of a fitting and banjo bolt.

...followed by the clip that holds it all together. Note the direction of the clip.

These are the components needed to plumb the master cylinder to the rear caliper. Never use anything other than approved brake line and fittings.

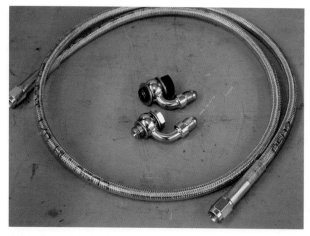

The front brake hose is a pretty simple deal. One hose, two fittings, four sealing washers.

This nifty banjo bolt/brake light pressure switch is a simple way to trigger the brake lights. Remember, with this set up they only work with the rear brakes.

BACK ON THE HOIST

Once Mike is finished with welding, the frame goes back on the hoist. The engine that's installed in the bike at this point is a 1994, 883 Sportster engine with five-speed transmission. This is the actual engine that will be used for this bike. When asked Frank says, "I paid twenty five hundred dollars for that engine, that's probably a pretty average price for a unit like that."

Frank points out the fact that there's a spacer right behind the drive sprocket. If you check the photos, you see that one of the spacers is thinner. This is the later model, which allows you to use a sprocket with a thicker and stronger hub.

At this point Frank and crew wrap up a number of small items. The upper motor mount, for example is two pieces. The link between the plate and the frame must be marked and drilled for a bolt. The forward controls are installed now, and the shift linkage is adjusted to put the lever at a comfortable position for the rider. As always, loctite is used on all of these mounting bolts.

Though the wiring sequence isn't included here, Frank passes on the following words of wisdom. "With a street fighter frame and a Buell you can use the Buell wiring harness and just pretty much plug everything in. The downside is the big connector junctions the factory harness uses, it's hard to hide those and you can't do as neat a job. Otherwise it's a nice simple way to wire the bike."

"With a chopper the factory harness isn't an option simply because the harness doesn't fit the longer frame and taller bars (especially if you use ape hangers and switches on the bars). Older Sportsters aren't a good choice for a harness either because everything connects in the headlight bucket, it's complicated to separate or connect and hide the wires, it's just not a good system."

After double checking the alignment a second time, Daniel gets a number 530 chain off the shelf runs it over the transmission sprocket and most of the rear sprocket to determine the length. Then the chain is put in the vise and "cut" (see photos) to the correct length. Finally the new chain is installed along with a master link, with the clip positioned as shown.

If the caliper is mounted so the bleeder is at the bottom, not the top, you may have to take the caliper off the bike for bleeding.

The mocked up machine, minus only wiring, paint and a few miscellaneous parts.

Left side shows off the vertical license plate bracket and taillight assembly, along with the trick and very expensive one-off seat.

No Waiting at Frank's Upholstery

The foam is one inch thick closed-cell insulation foam from the plumbing supply store. It's a good density and is readily available.

Cut the pieces oversize to start with (a serrated knife or turkey knife works well)...

...then spray the foam and the metal with spray trim adhesive. Next task is to stick the foam in place. Some situations (no pun intended)...

There are a a few parts of constructing a motorcycle that nearly every builder sends to an outside expert. These tasks include items such as paint, wiring (sometimes) and upholstery.

At Motorcycle Works, they like to do everything except paint. By doing it all in-house they save money - and time. An item often in short supply, especially if it's the night before the show.

As Frank illustrates. the process is pretty straightforward. The foam he uses is a bit of a find, as it's hard to get the correct foam at an upholstery or fabric store, "It's hard to get dense enough foam at the upholstery store," explains Frank. "The firmest foam they usually have in stock is RV foam and that isn't dense enough. We use a 1 inch Armaflex by Armstrong, it comes in several thicknesses. We use one-inch thick foam for our seats."

So head for the plumbing supply store and have at it.

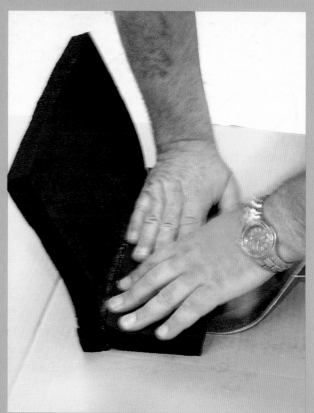

...like the back lower corner of this seat, require a second layer of foam, cut and installed just like the others.

No Waiting at Frank's Upholstery

Next comes the first trimming operation, using the metal edge as a guide...

Frank cuts another piece big enough to cover the entire metal seat base. Adhesive is applied to both surfaces again...

..followed by a little horizontal trim with the same serrated knife.

...before the big piece of foam is glued in place. The idea is to create a seat with thicker foam where you need it the most.

Fine tuning can be done with grinder, with a 40 grit pad. "But you have to be careful, the grinder will really cut the hell out of the foam."

After gluing on the big piece of foam Frank grinds the edges once more. Now we're ready for the vinyl covering.

The black vinyl can be purchased at a hobby store, upholstery supply house or fabric store. Rather than create a fold in the material...

Piece number 2 is cut big enough to overlap the first. Frank sprays adhesive as before, but this time he applies it to both pieces of vinyl.

...Frank decides to do this covering in 2 pieces. "This won't be a show quality seat, but is perfectly acceptable and will save you money."

Again, the vinyl is applied with plenty of tension so there are no wrinkles. Overspray adhesive can be cleaned up with Brake-Kleen.

The vinyl is applied with enough tension to eliminate any chance of wrinkles, then the folds in the back side are eliminated.

The finished seat. Like Frank says, "it's perfectly acceptable and saves you a couple of hundred dollars." And it took one hour, not one or two weeks.

A few more small items: The back of motor mount is threaded so regulator will mount there. The clutch cable is installed and adjusted per the service manual (see notes in Chapter Eight).

BRAKE LINES

For the front brake line they start with a line of the right length, then add the correct fitting on either end. The factory master cylinder uses a metric fitting while the aftermarket caliper is threaded to SAE specifications. All of this matching is no problem because the Goodridge brake line comes with a fitting on either end that matches up with the threads on an almost endless supply of possible hose-ends. After final assembly and bleeding you DO have to ensure all the junctions and fittings are tight and that there are no leaks.

The rear brake hose is installed much like the front. For a brake-light switch Frank puts a banjo bolt/switch combination right at the port coming off the master cylinder. You can hide the switch by using two shorter brake lines and installing the switch at the junction, but as Frank says, "that just creates more places for the brake fluid to leak."

Note, in order to utilize the brake light switch that's part of the factory front master cylinder you have to use the entire switch assembly, which was not done in this case. With the set up shown here there is no way to turn on the brake light with the front brake. Riders have to remember that the cars (and bikes) behind them only know they're on the brakes if they engage the rear brakes. These are all dash three hoses as mentioned in the brake section.

When all is said and done, Frank and crew have a very compact, usable chopper. A simple machine that didn't cost an arm and a leg. How much the final machine costs you depends on how much you spend on outside labor, fancy paint, and the latest trick accessories. Like Frank says, "The important thing is to buy a quality frame in the style you really want. Billet parts and accessories can come later as your budget permits."

A motley, though talented, crew. Left to right: Frank Pedersen, Mike Jensen, Noah Stotz, Daniel Valdez, Jeff Schneider.

Chapter Eight

Hillbilly Chopper

A Buell/Sportster Hardtail from Redneck

The project seen here is the construction of a Redneck Mutant Buell Conversion. These frames are designed to mate a Redneck hardtail chassis with a Buell engine and transmission.

The frame dimensions are two out and one

down, with a 40 degree rake at the neck. As Mike Marquart, manager at Redneck points out, "This set of dimensions works really well with a stock Buell fork while maintaining the look everyone wants. You can have the neck higher but of course

Sort of a before and after shot. The bike in the foreground is Mike Marquart's ride, the first completed Mutant Buell conversion, the outgrowth of Vince's original desire to build frames for Sportsters. In the rear is a Buell very similar to the donor bike Mike used to create the silver with flames back-to-basics beauty.

then the stock fork assembly won't work."

As this particular sequence illustrates you can easily use more than just the engine and transmission from the donor Buell. Fork, wheels, tires brakes, handlebar and controls can easily be used as well. Which makes this a very cheap chopper indeed.

The project starts with the disassembly of a 1997 Buell. Mike bought this bike for $2800, though he's quick to add, "Even $3500 would be a good price for this bike. Primarily we are going to use the engine, front end and wheels from this bike on our chopper project."

The deconstruction of the Buell is pretty straight forward and runs as follows. (Note, this sequence will differ slightly depending on the year and model of your Buell.) Sheet metal: The tail section can't come off 'till the tank is off or lifted up at least. There is wiring under the tank and tail section that must be unhooked before the tail section can be taken off completely. Battery: Be sure to unhook the negative cable first. In fact, unhooking the battery is probably the very first thing you should do. Exhaust: Take off the muffler, then the individual flange bolts and the header pipe itself.

Now Tim and Mikey loosen the engine bolts, disconnect the wiring to the engine and pull the top motor mount bracket off. The rest of the disassembly is probably better explained by the photos, but the sequence goes like this:

• Loosen the axle and slip the belt off the pulley.
• Remove the front belt guard.
• Loosen the top front motor mount..
• Take off the regulator.

Tim and Mike use a block of wood to keep the suspension from collapsing, then take out the rear shock bolt, followed by the front shock-engine mount bracket..

Now the shock can be removed completely. Drain the oil from the oil tank, this is another of those jobs that could have been done earlier.

It's important to separate and save the parts that will be reused. Like the regulator for example. Don't get hasty and start cutting wires during the disassembly. The boys do cut the oil lines however,

Tim and Mikey start with a perfectly serviceable Buell...

...disassembly goes quick and starts with the tail section and the tank.

Once the tail section and tank can be lifted up all the wires can be disconnected.

Mikey shoves a big timber under the rear subframe so the bike won't collapse...

...when the shock absorber is removed.

Taking things apart is the easy part and in less than an hour the engine is sitting on the floor.

explaining as they do, "it's OK, we're going to use all new lines anyway."

At this point the engine is loose in the bike, the wiring is disconnected and the motor is just about ready to pull out. Time now to take out three of the four rear mounting bolts. Eventually the only thing holding the engine in is one rear bolt and the front top mount assembly.

Rather than just drop and muscle the engine out of the chassis, a couple of wooden blocks are set up under the engine. Now Mikey can take out the front top bolts and the last rear bolt, so the engine comes to rest on the blocks. It becomes a matter of getting a couple of guys to pick the engine up briefly while the helper pulls the wood out and the engine comes to rest on the hoist.

After taking off the rear brake line Mikey picks up the bike so Tim can slip out the axle and then the rear wheel. After the two pivot bolts are out the swingarm is next (with a little help from a couple of pry bars).

The front end is next, the disassembly runs as follows:

- Loosen upper top clamp. Take the brake hose off at the master cylinder. Now the bars and speedometer come off
- At this point you can actually see the upper tree.
- Take off the big center nut.
- Lift off the upper tree.
- Lift up the frame.
- Take off the front end assembly.

ENGINE PREP

You need to do the clean up and prep work on the engine before installation with some carburetor cleaner or grease remover. Also, we need to pull the stud seen just below and ahead of the pulley.

Tim takes the bracket off the carburetor. Note the photos, the back of bracket is slotted. The nut on the rear breather only has to be loosened, not unscrewed completely.

Once the bracket is off Tim uses a Zinger or cut-off tool to trim off the bottom tab. Before reinstallation Tim and Mikey touch up the bracket with some black paint.

Tim puts Loctite on the 3 small Allens that mount the bracket to the mouth of the carburetor.

You have to thread a 3/8 inch coarse bolt into the hole at the very front of the case. It's a good idea to put pipe thread dope on these threads because they thread right into the case.

INSTALL AND ROUTE THE OIL LINES

Mikey and Tim mark the hoses, "supply and return." The new line is 5/16 inch fuel line rated for use with fuel injection.

Oil lines are much easier to install now than after the engine is in the new frame.
Wiring and electrical

As Mike Marquart explains: "We are replacing the ignition just to get rid of the external module the factory uses. If you were on a budget there's no reason you couldn't use the stock ignition and save yourself at least $200.00." Tim installs the ignition, setting the unit in the middle of its travel, the static timing will be set once the engine is in the frame.

The regulator bracket that comes with the frame requires that you drill two additional holes and matching holes in the front cross-member. As all these parts have already been painted it's a good idea to drill through a piece of masking tape to avoid tearing off any fresh paint. For the holes in the cross-member, Tim carefully drills holes a little more than half way through before carefully tapping the holes for 5/16 inch coarse fasteners.

The harness from Redneck is very simple, simple enough to be run inside the frame. Each harness includes provisions for a single-beam headlight, brake lights, coil and ignition, the rear taillight/brake light and the wire that energizes the starter solenoid (and three fuses). As Mike explains, "This is a simple harness, you can make up your own, but if you buy ours it comes with instructions and each end is numbered, which makes it pretty easy to install."

They install 2 upper wires, one to the coil, one to the headlight. Then taillight, brake light wires, and another group that drops down to the area where the battery box will be. The harness includes one extra wire that will be used later to

At this point there isn't much left except removal of the swingarm.

Swingarm removal is followed by disassembly of the front fork.

Here you can see the small carburetor bracket that must be cut off.

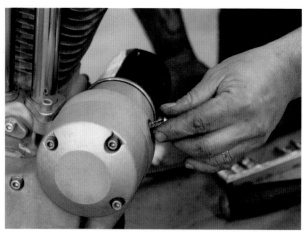

The empty hole in the front of the case goes right into the crank case, so it must be sealed with a bolt coated with sealer.

For the sake of a deadline, we decided to skip the mock-up and go directly from disassembled Buell to new chopper with painted frame and sheet metal.

The oil hoses are made up from 5/16 I.D. gas line clamped with chrome-plated, screw-type hose clamps.

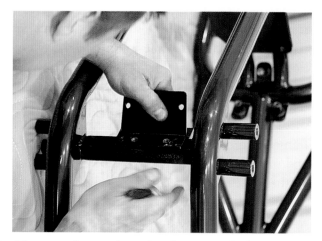

Tim uses the regulator bracket to mark the location of the mounting holes he will drill in the cross-member.

The line in his right hand is the feed line for the pump, it connects to the lowest point on the new oil tank.

The paint needs to be ground off the back of the regulator bracket where it bolts to the frame so the bracket, and the regulator will have a good ground.

pull the new ignition wires up through the frame tubes.

ENGINE INSTALL

It's easier to drop the frame down over the engine than to "install" the engine in the more conventional fashion. New through bolts are used at the front motor mount, though the old Buell bolts could certainly be used instead. Rear engine mounting bolts on the Buell are 7/16 inch for the top, 1/2 inch for the bottom. In fact, the holes on this frame need to be enlarged to accept the bigger Buell fasteners. You need to use the Buell washers on the rear motor mount bolts, standard round washers won't work. (Note: Sportsters use smaller diameter fasteners.) After all the bolts are started the whole affair is transferred to a stand and strapped in place.

Once the four rear bracket bolts are installed loosely it's time to install the left side bracket with two long bolts, then drop on the right side bracket. Tim gets all the bolts started then will pull them out one at a time, apply Loctite to each and reinstall them. All the bolts are gradually tightened up.

MORE FRAME PREP

Where the rear axle and spacers slide back and forth on the inside of the frame there's a raised area. As Tim explains, "you can easily have a .030 inch build up of paint on the inside of the frame and if you tighten the axle with that paint on there, the paint will squeeze out and then you have a loose axle. So we take a razor blade and carefully cut the paint off that raised area being careful not to peel off any more paint than we need to."

CONSTRUCTION CONTINUES

Installation of the oil tank is next but not before Mikey does a little preparation work. First he cleans all the threads on the tank, including the pipe threads on the bottom of the tank. And before installing the fittings Mikey blows compressed air through the tank itself to clear out any debris left from painting or manufacture.

A little out of sequence, this is the fork-stop bracket that will bolt to the lower triple tree.

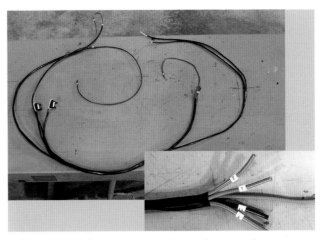

The Redneck harness is simple and relatively easy to install. Note that each end of the harness is marked.

Here Tim and Mikey pull the harness through the main tube of the frame.

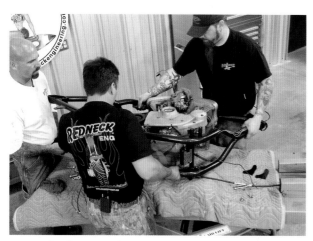

Instead of setting the engine in the frame, the frame is set over the engine.

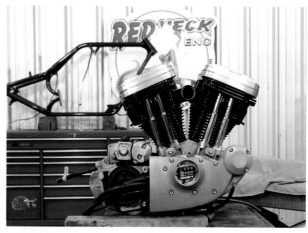

The finished motor, with painted cylinders and satin-finish covers. The covers were cleaned with carb cleaner then scuffed with a Scotch-Brite pad.

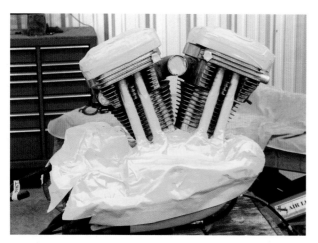

After the engine was installed, the crew decided it looked like hell. So they pulled it out again, cleaned and cleaned some more, then masked it off.

After putting on the carb, the aircleaner adapter is installed next.

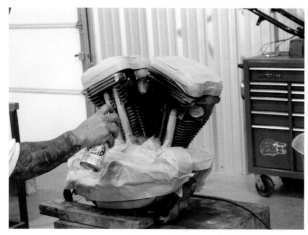

VHF spray paint is used to paint the cylinders. The key is a number of light coats so you get into all the cracks and crevices without any runs.

Mikey installs the oil tank before the rear wheel is put into place.

PLAN B

The motor that looked OK as part of the old Buell looks pretty shabby as part of a new chopper, surrounded by fresh paint. Tim, Mike and Mikey decide there's only answer. After pulling the engine again they spend a long evening cleaning everything with a scotch brite pad and some carburetor cleaner. With all the old grease and grime cleaned off they mask everything except the cylinders and use wrinkle finish paint from VHT to give the old girl a whole new look (VHT wrinkle Plus coating SP 201 black).

The following morning Tim is left with the job of installing the carburetor, a job that's made easier with a little WD 40 on the intake-manifold-grommet. Next comes installation of the bracket and the front air cleaner adapter

HOSE JOB

The vent hose is routed up and over the case then under the starter, and ends up clamped to either of the fittings on top of the oil tank. The ignition harness runs under the starter and under the oil tank. The oil feed line goes to the lowest point on the oil tank. This one (on the lower left of the oil tank) is hard to attach and clamp on the fitting. The oil return line goes to the other top fitting. Return and vent lines are run together up to the top of the tank, a 1/4 inch fastener is used as a guide to keep the hoses away from the pulley (note photos for details on routing).

INSTALL REAR WHEEL AND FENDER

Tim holds the fender up while Mikey starts the two top bolts. To minimize damage to the new paint small fiber washers are used between the fender and frame to avoid tearing up the paint (these can be purchased at many auto and hardware stores). Before final tightening of the fender bolts the axle is put in place so the back of the bike will be at its final dimension. Sometimes there's enough paint build up in the area where the axle blocks slide that a little material has to be taken off the axle block itself.

Now the rear wheel is installed for the first time. Because there was no a mock-up it's necessary to measure for the wheel spacers now. First the wheel is installed with the belt in place, then

This photo shows the routing of the oil hoses and how a 1/4 inch bolt was uses as a guard to keep the hoses away from the sprocket.

Installation of the rear fender starts from underneath - the bolts screw in from the inside into the short frame stubs.

The rear wheel needs to be installed and then removed more than once so Tim can align the wheel and check for spacers.

Tim adjusts belt for tension, and positions the wheel so the belt tracks straight and stays in the middle of the pulley when the wheel is rotated forward.

All the spacers at Redneck are cut from stainless steel tubing stock.

Then he measures for the spacer on each side.

With the spacers in place the axle can be installed for the last time.

Once a spacer is cut Tim checks the dimension.

This short link is what keeps the caliper from going 'round and 'round when you step on the brake.

A correctly positioned wheel will keep the belt in the middle of the pulley when the wheel is rotated in a forward direction.

the axle adjusters are used to put tension on the belt. Tim is happy with the way the belt tracks if he can spin the wheel in a forward direction and the belt stays in the center of the pulley without crowding over to one side. He uses a simple mechinist's rule to measure the distance from the outside of the wheel bearing to the inside of the frame (note the pictures). Mikey marks the axle block position in the frame so it's easy to re-align the rear wheel.

After Mikey cuts a spacer from stainless stock the wheel comes off again, the spacers are held in place and the axle is slipped through again. When everything is re-positioned the belt is tensioned and the wheel position is checked one last time. The axle adjusting bolts are two different lengths, the long bolt is used on the drive side and the

As explained in the text, one adjusting bolt is longer than the other. Small lock-Allens are screwed down on top of the adjusting bolts.

This is the special battery used with Redneck frames, small enough to fit in the lower battery tray.

After being routed through the top tube, wires to the ignition switch, and ignition components are separated and grouped into shrink wrap.

After being routed into shrink wrap, a little heat makes the tubing, well, shrink, and creates a harness that looks like "factory."

This is one of three in-line fuse holders used with the Redneck harness.

Here are the two groups of wires prior to wiring the ignition switch and coils.

License plate bracket attaches with a single bolt, wires are routed into the frame tubes.

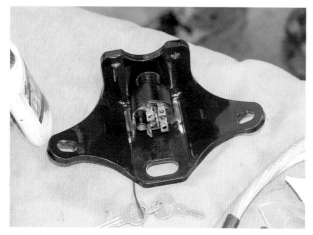

The switch itself is screwed into the switch housing and motor-mount bracket before any wires are attached.

After attaching the wires to the switch, Tim makes sure the switch is tight in the bracket.

short one on the left because the bolt for the license plate bracket screws into the left side adjusting hole.

A short linkage made up from two Heim joints is used to lock the rear caliper in place. "We make these up," explains Mike, "but you could probably use one of the links off the Buell motor mount." Once the link is in place both sides of the axle can be tightened.

MORE WIRING

This frame kit uses a "builder's battery" that is slightly smaller than the stock battery (Deka ETX 12). The battery tray is a Redneck item that comes with the frame. The battery cables are made up from 4 gauge welding cable but most individuals working at home will simply buy them (negative cable is 12 inches long, the positive is 16 inches long).

The battery box bolts into the frame and fits very tight. In fact, to get the battery and tray in place requires at least three hands, two to hold the battery under the bike while the third slips the tray underneath and up into place so the two bolts can be screwed in place from the bottom, into the cross-member.

At this time the ignition wires were pulled up through the main top tube, using the extra "tag" wire that was pulled through the tube earlier. They emerge at the upper motor mount bracket and are joined up with the other parts of the harness there.

The upper mount can go on now, but first the ignition switch needs to be mounted. Tim threads it into the bracket, this is an automotive type switch with a spring loaded start position. The Redneck harness does not use a separate starter button, or a starter relay between the ignition switch and the starter solenoid. The coil being used here is from Crane, designed to work with the HI-4 ignition. Once the ignition switch is in Tim can connect the wires to the back of the Crane coil, and mount the coil to the bracket.

There are 3 wires at the positive battery terminal: one from regulator, the battery cable, and the main feed wire for the rest of the harness, (this wire includes a fuse holder for a 30 amp fuse). In the same area there are two wires for the brake

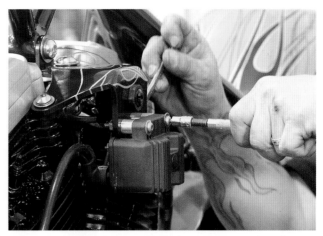

The single-fire Crane coils bolt to the same bracket as the ignition switch.

The levers are adjusted for good leverage, and to put the shifter at a comfortable position.

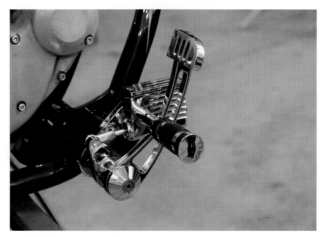

Right side forward control and master cylinder mount like they would on any soft-tail.

1. Installation of the fork stop collar starts by pressing the stem out of the lower tree.

2. Holes are then drilled and tapped...

3....so the collar can be installed. Next the stem is pressed back in...

4....and the lower bearing is reinstalled (after bring packed).

5. Now the lower tree can be pushed up into place, the top tree dropped on, and the nut tightened.

6. Before the final tightening of the top nut can occur, Tim and Mikey work the tubes down into the trees until they are flush with the top of the top tree.

Once the tubes are flush with the top of the top tree, and the lower pinch bolts are tight, the stem nut can be tightened per Tim's comments in the text.

The brackets for the small fairing must be installed at the same time as the headlight.

Installing the front fender is pretty simple, but don't try to do it if the wheel is already in place.

light switch (these will be run forward to the brake light switch on the master cylinder) and one for the starter solenoid. Note: this harness uses no horn,or hi-low switch, but other harnesses from Redneck do utilize both.

As mentioned earlier, the license plate housing bolts on with one fastener that goes into the same hole as the axle adjuster on the left side. Then the two wires are connected with butt connectors and shrink wrap to seal the connection. The taillight grounds through the bracket though you could run a separate ground wire.

FORWARD CONTROLS

The forward controls used here are standard soft-tail style controls. Though frames can be ordered without the forward controls, with rear sets, or whatever the customer wants. On the left

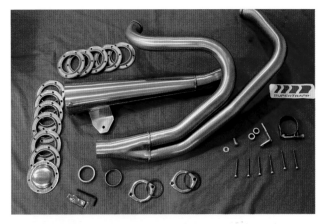

Supertrapp exhaust and lots of discs are the exhaust system of choice for Redneck Mutant Buells. Be sure the exhaust mounting plate is in place before the frame is painted.

Here you can see the vent and filter for the transmission, and two in-line fuse holders.

Before installing the exhaust, the flanges must be installed. Full-size factory exhaust gaskets are used because they do a better job of sealing.

Mikey starts at the front pipe, positioning the header pipe, then the flange, then the two 5/16 inch nuts.

side Mikey takes the shift lever off the shaft and the control assembly apart to get a better angle on the two levers. Next the right side master cylinder assembly goes on the bike.

Now Tim checks for the brake line length and the necessary fittings. Goodridge makes the banjo bolt with the integral switch. The line installation starts at the back, Mikey uses the factory banjo bolt with metric threads, a new set of sealing washers is often a good idea. The lines are routed under the bike to the rear master cylinder.

FRONT END PREPARATION AND ASSEMBLY

This is one of those multi-step operations and goes like this:

- Take the headlight brackets off the tubes, take off the lower tree.
- Force out the bearing and dust shield.
- Press out the stem.
- Drill and tap for fork lock.
- Install fork lock.
- No dust shield.
- Install the stem. When you reinstall the stem, there's a groove for the fork lock on the Buell, but the Redneck frame doesn't use that, so the position of the groove doesn't matter (in a radial sense).
- Pack the neck bearings and install.
- Put lower tree back on tubes, in about same position as before.
- Headlight brackets go on now.
- Put front end on bike, loosely install top tree.
- Snug the lower tree pinch bolts.
- Snug the top nut.

The Redneck neck is different dimension than stock, so the tubes stick up through the top tree (those pinch bolts are loose too).

Now loosen lower-tree pinch bolts, and gently tap the tubes down so they are flush with upper tree

With upper bolt tight, tighten all pinch bolts. Now tighten and adjust the upper bolt - you are in fact adjusting the stem bearings. "I like to tight-

92

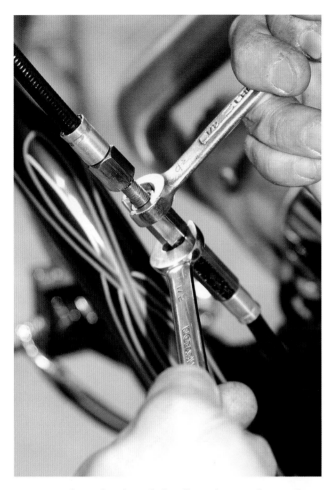

By extending the threaded collars that make up this clutch adjusting assembly you essentially make the cable shorter and reduce free play.

en it until you get just a little resistance to the back and forth movement of the fork," explains Tim, "so it doesn't just flop but still turns nice and smooth."

After correctly adjusting the upper nut the position of the bolt is locked with the pinch bolt (check the photos). In order to reinstall the front fender the wheel has to come out of the fork assembly.

INSTALL THE FAIRING AND HEADLIGHT

Pull the headlight out of the bucket, then wire the headlight. No ground wire is used, the black wire from the bulb is run right to a bolt on the bucket. Mikey drills a hole in the bucket so the headlight wire comes into the bucket at a better angle.

Before installing the gas tank it's a good idea

Once the header pipes are in place, with the nuts screwed loosely on the studs, the muffler assembly can be slipped into place.

Once the clutch cable is hooked up and adjusted you have to work it a few times to ensure all the parts are seated. Lubing the cable is another good idea.

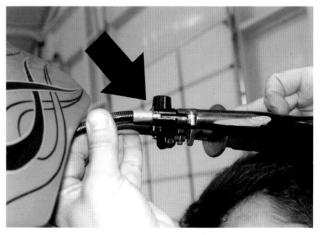

A correctly adjusted clutch should have 1/16th to 1/8th inch of play where the cable ferrule goes into the lever assembly.

93

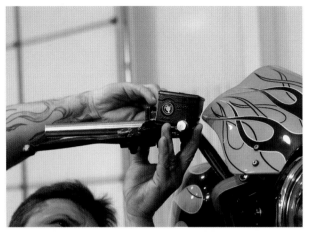

Here Tim attaches the master cylinder to the bars. All of this is easier as the whole front end was borrowed from the Buell.

...with the pull cable in the outside ferrule.

A small Allen wrench is essential for assembling the throttle assembly.

The brake hose and ends are new, everything else came off the Buell.

The throttle cables run as shown...

When installing the clip, it's best to be careful and always use a guard on the drill bit.

to flush it out with a little gas or at least compressed air. You also need to clean the threads in the mounting holes with a tap. The problem with not doing a mock-up crops up now, when the upper part of the triple tree is found to contact the tank at full lock in either direction. Tim resolves the problem by removing a bit of metal from the top of the speedo mount/upper clamp. Once the tank is in place the gas line can be routed across the top of the engine to the carburetor.

The breather hoses are next, first the 5/16 inch line is run from the transmission vent over to the left side of the bike, where it's attached to the small chrome vent/filter assembly, which is simply tie-wrapped in place. The head-breather hoses are routed to the front of the engine, behind the oil filter and down under the engine. New 3/8 inch hose is used for all 3 vents.

Install Exhaust

First it's necessary to slide the flanges on the pipes. Next come the big snap rings, then the header pipes go on the engine using new 5/16 fine thread nuts.

Hangin' the header pipes is one of those jobs that requires patience. It's a matter of holding the pipes in place while you get a nut started. Before he's done Mike drops the nuts and lock washers a number of times.

Controls and Cables

We are using the old Buell controls here. After the clutch cable is adjusted there should be 1/16 to 1/8 inch free play where the cable ferrule sets into the lever assembly, so you know the clutch isn't dragging. This adjustment may have to be readjusted in 500 miles if you've installed a new cable (due to cable stretch).

Throttle cables are routed under the tank at the front, over the top mount and across to the carburetor. The pull cable goes to the outside cable ferrule and the return cable goes to the inside position.

Adjust the pull cable to the point where it pulls the throttle all the way open, then "just take the play out of the return cable," explains Tim. Now the boys install the seat clip with two pop rivets. It's an easy job, but they both warn, "use

Pop rivets hold the clip to the seat base.

Nifty little aircraft-style gas cap screws into standard threads in tank...

...with two brass plugs to give the installer leverage.

Two and a half quarts of oil are added before firing the engine for the first time.

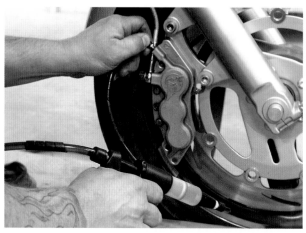

Here Tim has it hooked up to the front bleeder, and he pumps until...

Primary/transmission fluid is added until the level meets the bottom of the clutch basket.

...the reservoir is full and no more bubbles emerge.

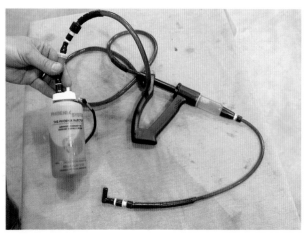

This pump is used to bleed the brakes by filling from the bleeder end.

Rear brakes are bled in the same way...

aguard on the drill bit or oops, you've drilled right through the seat."

FLUIDS

The standard Buell oil tank holds 2-1/4 quarts, the Redneck tanks hold about 2-1/2, so Mikey puts in about 2-1/2 quarts and will check the level after the engine is run for a few minutes. Before putting in new fluid the boys drain out all of the old primary/transmission fluid. New fluid is installed until it reaches the bottom of the clutch basket, just like a big twin.

As mentioned elsewhere in this tome, bleeding brakes is one of those operations that should be easy but sometimes isn't. Tim and Mikey use a system that forces the fluid in from the bleeder, the whole thing goes like this:

Open the bleeder. Pump fluid in until the reservoir is full. Close the bleeder. They try the lever and find no resistance at all, the lever goes right up against the bar. Only after pumping the lever numerous times does it begin to develop any meaningful pressure.

For the rear brakes the boys go through the same procedure, Tim explains that "sometimes the rear is harder, because the whole system is at the same level, the air wants to rise but there's no place for it to rise to." But in actuality the rear pedal is hard on the first try.

THE IMPORTANCE OF THE TEST RIDE

Each Redneck bike gets three separate test rides by three different riders, before being turned over to the customer. First Tim takes it out on the standard loop, then any little problems are fixed or adjusted and all the bolts are checked to be sure they're tight. Then Mikey (or another mechanic) takes it out and goes through the same process. Finally, Mike Marquart takes it out for the final road test and signs off.

Thought it was conceived as a budget bike, what Vince and the crew at Redneck have created is simply a very cool little hardtail. It might be a way to do something more exciting with that Sportster in the garage, a way to build a budget Chopper, or a way to have an inexpensive bar-hopper. - the choice is up to you.

...until the master cylinder reservoir is filled and bubble free.

Does it run?

Yes, it runs like a Redneck.

Chapter Nine

Klocker Chopper

A $30,000 bike for only about $15,000

Brian Klock is one of those young men who seem to come out of no where, suddenly appearing in the center of all the action, on every magazine cover on the news stand.

Actually, Brain is from a little town near Mitchell, South Dakota and today his shop is located in Mitchell. Quick to pick up on a trend, or help create one of his own, Brian's success is based on persistence (he's been in business since 1997) and skill, and just goes to show that you

You don't have to spend thirty thousand dollars to create a stunning chopper. This machine from Klock Werks combines a new-from-the-dealer Sportster engine their own frame, wire wheels and a great paint job.

don't have to have an L.A. address to be successful.

One of Brian's newest projects is a Sportster based chopper frame designed in conjunction with Marc Rowe. The sequence that follows documents construction of the second chopper to be built with the new frame (with a few images borrowed from other, similar, projects). The copy that follows is Brian's, as are all the captions and most of the photographs.

STYLE

Sportsters were big in the 1970s and early 1980s because they were affordable and you could modify them within a budget. The same holds true today. Buying a damaged or cosmetically well worn Buell or Sportster for a price of 3K to 5K will allow you to spend $10K on parts to achieve a $30,000 look for only 13K to 15K. It just makes sense – for many it may mean taking their first ever bike and converting it into a dream project while retaining the sentimental value.

The key to building a bike cheap or expensive is assembling the correct components. Know what the big picture is so you can stay in the lines – like coloring as a kid. A small-tired bike can outshine a big tire or a big motor given the right selection of parts, color and stance.

Most of the images used here come from the - "warthog" of Mark Missildine in it's Burple coat with hot rod flames.

This is Klock Werks' exclusive rubbermount chopper frame for Sportsters. It has 6" of stretch in the downtubes and 2" in the backbone while the neck rake is set at 40. We strongly recommend using a six degree triple tree for the correct trail.

Along with the swingarm and frame, the customer will receive (R to L, top to bottom) a rear engine mounting block, top motor mount, front engine plate mounts, rear hidden axle, Dyna mounting block for the front of motor and aluminum rear fender struts.

This photo shows the aluminum strut with blind drilled holes for fender mounting and tapered allens to affix the struts to the frame.

The cleveblock, isolator bushing and washer need to be installed using JIMS tool part #DS-196067.

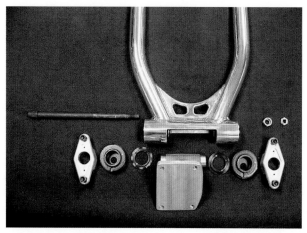

This photo shows the pivot shaft, cleveblocks and isolator washer from H-D, along with the pivot blocks, swingarm and rear engine support plate.

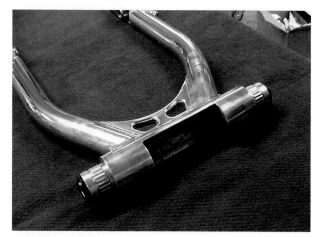

Align the cleveblocks with the washer and isolator bushing installed.

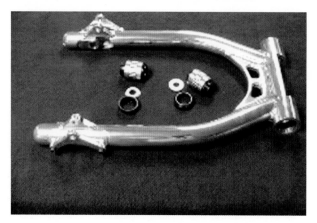

The swingarm can be painted or polished per your choice. The rubbermount isolators will need to be purchased for an FXR, we recommend using genuine Harley Davidson parts here.

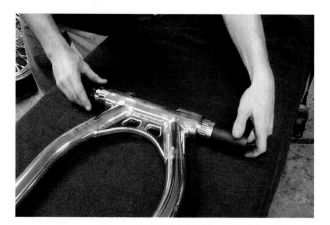

Insert JIMS cleveblock Installation Tool keeping things centered and snug.

Style doesn't come in dollars – a good eye can make a pile of junk flow well together. Compile what you like and follow it through.

PAINT, THINK & PLAN

Paint can make or break any bike. Don't just have your Uncle do it because he can. Money well spent on quality here will win shows and definitely influence people. Keep in mind that bright colors photograph well if you are in pursuit of a magazine spread.

Think the whole project through. If you clip out 10 choppers from magazines that are six inches up and one that is eight – go find a chassis that is six inches up and try it on for size. Don't build for the trend, build for yourself and execute properly no matter what you are creating. Diversity is the spice of motorcycling and life!

BARS, SEAT, TANK

Handlebars and the seat are always last – don't rush this purchase. Try a few sets of bars or mock up some $10 swap meet specials, cut them and tack weld to get a custom look. You'll be money ahead and it will greatly shape the stance of the bike.

Sportster tanks have been the basis for countless chopper builds over the years. The 1998 and newer tanks with the rounded bottoms bode well for the smoothness of many of today's bikes – while the straight bottom promotes the old school style that is happening. These tanks can be picked up dented or scratched at any swap meet or on ebay. Reposition the tank filler neck or use a different style. Cut the tunnel to mount it down low or raise it for the "Frisco" attitude. No matter the size of the bike – these tanks look great – don't overlook them on your way to a chopper with style.

STYLE/EASE OF BUILD

Sportster motors make great starter bikes for builders of all levels. The motor, transmission and primary are one piece. No alignment problems, the entire drivetrain can be assembled in the frame in one swift move. Be it a rigid, soft-tail or a rubber-mount the entire package is one step. Start with a bike that ran and worked – then it's only a matter of wiring that could downplay your instant success.

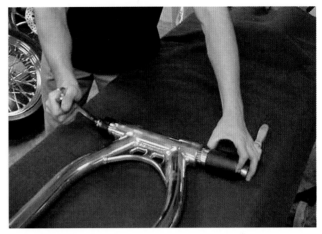

Tim Wagner tightens the cleveblocks to flush with the outside edges of the swingarm.

Tim installs the pivot blocks after the swingarm has been filled with the proper parts.

Phil Hurd holds the swingarm while Tim torques down the pivot blocks.

The blocks will be polished later but have been left raw to ease mock up and avoid scratches.

Tim installs the sprocket and rotors using loctite and the proper torque sequences so they are ready for fitment.

Dan Cheeseman installs the rear axle and wheel before bolting up the shocks in preparation for rear fender mounting.

Dan installs the neck races using the correct size driver tool and a mallet. Then he will pack the bearings and install them with the triple tree.

In South Dakota bikes are not required to have turn signals so the wiring is minimal. The "warthog" project (blue bike) was for a customer in Georgia so the signals were a prerequisite. The ProOne trees provided a style and look we were after in front while the Lazer star lights in the rear serve as running lights and signals for added visibility and safety. You can have functionality and style. Be patient, exhaust your resources and think creative while maintaining workable parameters for the components you've chosen. Don't sacrifice.

FRAME

The frame we designed with Marc Rowe ended up looking like a bike he had in 1970 because of the boxed backbone area. Marc said he fell in love with my drawing but wouldn't say why. Upon receiving the production version of the frame he called and told me to un-pack the neck which con-

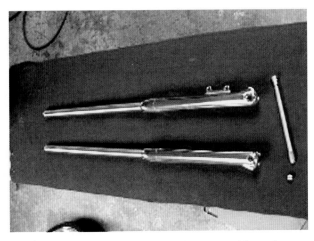

H-D Deuce legs were purchased in assemblies, then 10" over tubes swapped for stock. They are filled, ready to install using a Dakota Billet flush axle.

Tim has applied a silicone based lubricant to the tubes to avoid any marring as he installs them into the trees.

Many states require the use of signals. Pro-one offers these trees in a raked version with built in signals.

The Dakota Billet axle is in place as we install the wheel, rotor and caliper. Be sure everything is centered and spaced correctly before fitting the fender.

Tim installs the steering stem and torques it into place while Dan keeps the top from turning.

The ten over tubes, deuce legs, flush axle and raked trees are giving us the chopper look with the smooth style we were after.

We tape a guide to the wheel for fender fitment - a broken drive belt - but a piece of hose will work. Leave plenty of clearance at this point. Consider fender spacers and fork braces that will be added.

You can see we have raised the tank and mounted the tunnel much lower on the stock frame.

The radius follows the rim, clean and smooth!

Utilizing a Ness headlight or stock HD style can save big money over billet counter parts. Consider painting the outer shell and leaving ring chromed.

Utilizing a stock Sportster tank we cut the tunnel and mounted it high to show off the boxed back-bone and motor mount. Note the tucked in mount of the headlight.

The oil tank and mounting tabs were supplied with the frame. Updated tanks now fill the gap because of stylized side panels. (See next photo)

Fender mounts must allow clearance when swingarm is bottomed out. Test with shocks unhooked. Once satisfied with clearance, mark and cut side radius on fender to match rim, tire lines. This is a before picture.

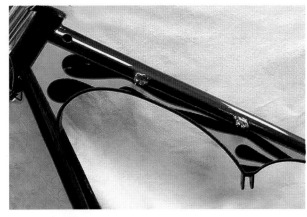

As we go to final assembly – you can get a good look at the flush mount tank tabs we utilized. They accept stock rubber grommets and sleeves.

Here is the bike in full mockup – note the lack of handlebars, make sure they fit you and the look.

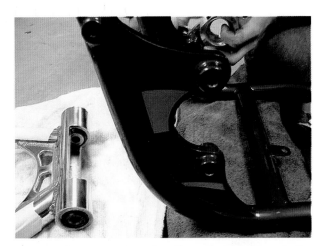

Notice the attention to detail on the paint work. In the upper left hand section we have welded bungs on to the frame to accommodate passenger pegs.

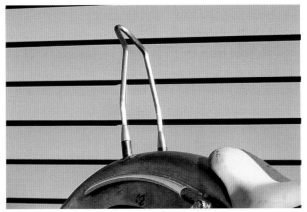

The rear sissy bar is a custom piece the crew at Klock Werks bent up. We welded the mounting points to the rear fender. Be sure and brace it properly underneath to avoid flex.

The holes in the frame are used to hide throttle cables and wiring and need to be drilled before painting.

A new 1200 motor straight from Harley Davidson anxiously awaits being attached to the boxed motor mount.

Dan & Tim assemble the oil tank. All pieces are test fit – judging paint build up can be tricky.

Tim overlooks the tabs on the frame to make sure all ground surfaces are clean and the motor can be installed.

The swingarm pivots are fully polished. Note the difference chrome hardware can make on your build. Don't overlook the details.

tained a scanned copy of his bike! What a surprise – sometimes things just connect. This also goes to show you that the more things change – style stays the same. It all comes full circle eventually.

The bike uses an FXR-style mounting block in the rear and a Dyna motor mount in the front to allow a smoother ride and retain the stock length (12 inch) shocks from the original donor bike.

The oil tank is available through us and we also have a soft-tail style available. The 180 rear tire is the correct size for a Sportster motor in this case as it's a modern size with a classic look. Early choppers didn't have 250 or 300 tires.

The motor chrome is masked off and Dan and Tim install the whole assembly. You can't be too careful at this stage. Take your time and protect all surfaces.

The crew fabbed up a custom exhaust for this bike per the customer's request. We "fish mouthed" the tips, did our final welding and put the rush on Deter's polishing in Minneapolis.

Note the new style oil tank wings and drive pulley. In subsequent photos you'll notice we modified the cover to clean up the look. The details are the key!

The flames are carried under the seat for solo use, always a good idea. Struts are polished and the fender has its final radius in view.

The paint detail in the neck adds to the design of the bike. Note that a softail style oil tank could be used and would lend a modern look.

The sissy bar is back from chrome. Again look at the radius of the fender. The 180 rear tire fits well and will handle great. 12 inch works shocks are being used on this project.

The custom tweak bar or fork brace keeps the front end from twisting. The fender spacers are integrated and this piece is available from Klock Werks for Deuce front ends.

Wimmer Machine upswept air cleaner lends a sense of style and height while maintaining function.

The project is coming together. The flames, tank mounting and custom headlight placement are all very evident.

Look at that gem shine! Note the sprocket cover, final pipe finish and seat profile.

Neck to tank detail and gas tank filler, all add to the feeling of height on this bike.

Dan has a thing for motor mounts so he fabbed this one. Choke knob is a firing pin that was saved from a diffusion performed by the Navy Seal who owns the bike, Mike Missildine.

The lazer star lights look right at home, Tim hid the wiring and they serve as running lights and signals.

You can see in this picture how we prefer to route the oil lines. Don't forget about being creative with that sprocket cover as well.

Dan and Tim install the wiring to the Performance Machine switches. Everything was run internally to keep things clean.

Just add mirrors – clean looking controls and bars – just what Mark ordered.

The Dakota Digital Speedo is integrated into the Klock Werks Bars. The gas cap houses a Winchester medallion from Mark's dad who was a world champion skeet shooter. Did I mention the details…

Tim finalizes the throttle adjustment before firing it up for a test ride.

The lines of the trees, headlights and bars all work in symmetry to create the stance. The gauge cup and headlight work well together. We utilize black lines – so as not to draw attentions. Cables are not pretty.

The 180 looks sizeable and the classic chopper stance was achieved.

Yes, It's a Sportster!

The always moving Mr. Klock with his creation at a bike show in Daytona Beach (not many palm trees in Mitchell, South Dakota).

Chapter Ten

Perewitz Big Twin

Least Cheap of the Cheap Choppers

PART ONE, THE MOCK-UP

Before the Perewitz crew can screw together this big twin chopper they have to do a mock-up to ensure everything fits and all the necessary brackets are installed before the paint is applied. Most of the mock-up is done by Ron Landers, with help from in-house machinist Jack Morrison.

MOUNT THE GAS TANK

One of Ron's first tasks is the manufacture of tank-mounting brackets. This is probably about a

It's not a kit. Just carefully chosen parts that will give us the chopper look we're after, without breaking the bank. You don't have to use the parts we did. A Santee frame (to name just one) could be substituted for the Redneck item, and a Harley 80 inch Evo substituted for the RevTech. Be sure you buy a quality frame, though.

four hour job to cut all of them from a sheet of mild steel and then grind each one to fit the frame and tank precisely. This is one more item you're going to have to deal with or allow for in the budget. Maybe another reason to order a complete rolling chassis kit with sheet metal ready for installation.

Anyway, each of the four small brackets are made by hand. After the brackets are fabricated Ron bolts them to the bottom of the tank, snugs up the mounting bolts and tack welds them to the frame's top tube.

Ron spends time choosing exactly the best spot for the tank to sit...

The Major Parts

Redneck hardtail frame
ProOne 41mm fork assembly
Ness handle bars
CCI handle bar controls
BDL Belt Drive
RevTech 88 inch engine & 5-speed tranny
DNA laced wheels
Avon tires, 90/90X21 front, 250X18 rear
Billet Concepts forward controls
Perewitz license plate bracket/mounting kit
GMA 4-piston calipers and rotors
Samson exhaust
Wernimont fenders
CCI gas tank
Spyke starter

...before fabricating the four mounting tabs and screwing them to the bungs already installed in the bottom of the tank.

INSTALL ENGINE.

Ron and George use an "engine lifting tool" that screws onto the left end of the crank to make it easier to lift and install the heavy V-twin engine. For the mock-up Ron uses common Grade 5 bolts and will substitute chrome bolts on the final assembly.

Ron explains that, "I like to install the inner primary, snug up the primary-to-engine and primary-to-tranny bolts, then check and see how much the engine and tranny move around in the frame with the mounting bolts loose." Next Ron installs a rear wheel and belt though the final alignment will be done a little later, as we don't have the right wheel at this time.

Then it's time to tack weld the tabs to the frame, take off the tank and do the final welding with the tig welder.

Once the engine is in place Ron can set the 5-speed transmission in the frame...

Here you can see how Ron cut a wide tab out of the Wernimont fender to provide belt clearance.

...followed by the first installation of the BDL engine/transmission plate. Ron tightens the plate-to-engine and tranny bolts before he tightens up the engine and tranny mounting bolts.

Like the front, the rear fender can't be positioned too close to the tire or the tire will grow at speed and rub on the bottom of the fender.

Ron puts in a wheel similar to what will eventually be used (but hasn't arrived yet) just so the fender can be mounted.

To give the fender more strength without using conventional struts, Ron cuts and installs these reinforcing plates to the inside of the fender.

REAR FENDER

Ron explains that, "The rear fender is a blank from Russ Wernimont and must be cut out to clear the belt. I like to mark the area I'm going to cut with a marker, then line it with tape, just because the tape edge is so much easier to follow with the cut-off wheel." Ronnie also installs reinforcing blanks on the inside of the fender as shown in the nearby photos. These are cut from larger pieces of curved 1/4 inch mild steel plate and then welded to the inside of the fender.

INSTALL FRONT END

Once the two triple trees are installed the two fork tubes are screwed up into the top trees. Because the tubes screw up into the upper tree the standard upper caps don't work. ProOne supplies brass plugs that are used to cap off the tubes. These are three-degree trees used to reduce the amount of trail to a more reasonable level.

David explains, "When it comes to figuring out how long the front end should be, there is a table, but over the years I've learned to just judge it from experience."

1. The ProOne tubes screw up into the upper trees for a clean look. Once in place the lower pinch bolt can be tightened.

2. Tapered bearings require set up prior to installation. First the bearings need to be packed (if you haven't done it let the shop do it), then the whole thing must be assembled.

3. With an axle in the vise the wheel, bearings and center spacer are installed.

4. Once assembled the end play is checked with a dial indicator. First check shows .025 inches, the second shows a much better .004 inches.

115

David helps as Ron slides in the front axle.

Blueing or "dykem" makes it easier to see the scribe marks. Short studs and temporary spacers are used during this mock-up session.

Aluminum spacers are used to center the wheel between the fork tubes.

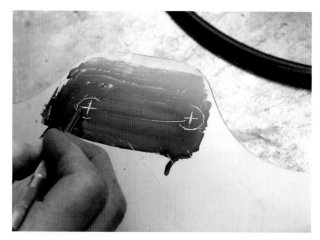

Now the center of the two mounting holes can be determined.

Ron and Dave take time deciding exactly where the front fender should mount. Rubber tubing keeps the fender up off the tire during the mock-up.

A template is used to create a nice smooth curve.

Wheels, Wheel Bearings and Adjustments

The 21 inch front wheel from DNA uses the older-style tapered wheel bearings. Jesse Perewitz gets the job of setting up the bearings for the correct end play. When first checked the free play measures .025 inch with the spacer installed. The factory recommends .002 to 006 inches with the axle nut tightened to 50 ft. lbs. In order to reduce end play Jesse machines 021.inches off the inner spacer, which moves the bearings closer together and gives him a new measurement of .004 inches.

Obviously, if there had been little or no end play Jesse would have added shims to the central spacer to increase the end play. Shims are available from any good dealership or aftermarket shop. Also, PTI makes an adjustable center spacer that eliminates the need for shims or grinding, available from Drag Specialties. Note: If you buy wheels with the bearings already installed, you have to be sure that they are actually packed with grease, and that the end play is within specification. This is one of those things that sounds too obvious to mention, but we know someone who's new front wheel stopped wheeling recently resulting in a bad spill. All because of dry bearings.

Install the Front Fender

Ron starts the mock-up of the fender by placing a piece of hose on the tire and then placing the fender on the hose, explaining as he does, "You have to leave room for the tire to grow at speed, otherwise once you're on the highway the tire will burn the paint off the fender, or worse." The position of the front fender has a huge impact on the bike's looks and lines, and Ronnie spends considerable time determining the best position for the fender.

Next he puts a set of studs in the lower legs and a temporary set of spacers because the real spacers haven't been manufactured yet. Ron then trims the excess metal off the mounting tab on either side of the fender. For this he uses a template made earlier (note the photos).

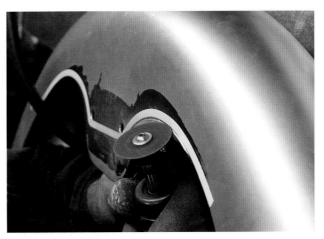

Ron likes to use tape to outline the curves as it's easier to see than the scribed line.

Handle bars are seldom round. Ron has to remove metal on the high areas...

...so the control assemblies will slide on.

The first installation of the rear wheel puts the axle at the forward end of its travel...

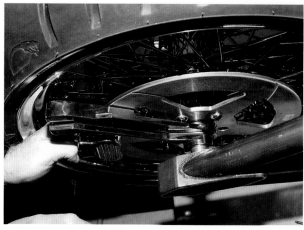

Before measuring for spacers you have to decide where the caliper carrier will be positioned...

...a situation that is remedied by the installation of a 135 tooth belt (instead of only 132).

...and then measure for a spacer...

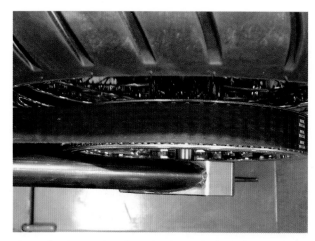

David adjusts the the wheel until the belt is tight enough and runs in the middle of the pulley as the wheel is turned in a forward direction.

...on both sides of the caliper carrier.

The handle bars go on now, Ron slides on the controls and discovers that the bars aren't exactly round where the controls mount. This requires a little corrective action with the small grinder and a 36 grit pad.

REAR WHEEL ALIGNMENT

Before the wheel can be installed, the 70 tooth pulley and then the rotor must be installed. The rear caliper bracket from GMA has only a 3/4 inch hole for the axle and must be enlarged to accept the 1 inch axle used with this rear wheel.

When Ron and Dave install the rear wheel for the first time they discover that the belt is just barely long enough and the axle is at the forward end of the adjustment slot. In most cases the frame manufacturer will specify the length of the belt and the size of the rear pulley that should be used. This frame may have been designed for a 132 tooth belt and 65 tooth pulley instead of the 70-tooth pulley Ron installed. In any case, this is a good example of things that go wrong in the real world and why the mock-up is such a good idea. "The reason I want to use the 70 Tooth sprocket," explains Dave, "is this bike only has an 88 inch motor, the bigger sprocket will give it more low end power. It ain't a 90 mph cruiser by any means so the lower gearing will give it better acceleration in town." Ron pulls the wheel back out, removes the inner primary and installs the new 135 tooth belt.

ALIGNMENT OF FINAL-DRIVE BELT

David starts by getting the belt snug (this wheel uses sealed bearings). Next, he adjusts the wheel to get the belt to track well. The belt should not twist or run up against either side of the rear pulley when the wheel is rotated in a forward direction. "We keep the belt as close as we can to the tire," explains Dave. "Then check the tire visually to make sure it's in the middle of the frame, but pretty much the tire position is determined by the position of the transmission pulley."

With the wheel and tire where they should be Jack measures for the three spacers that must be

To measure for the left side spacer Jack first uses a snap gauge as shown, and will add the distance from the wheel bearing to the pulley after the wheel is out.

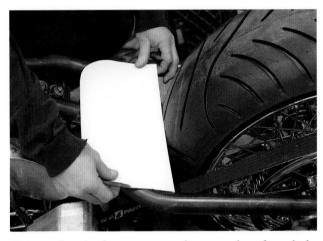

Ron makes the front support plate template from light board...

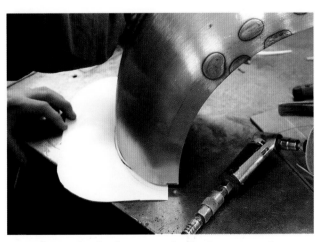

...and uses the fender to mark the concave section.

After a test fit of the template...

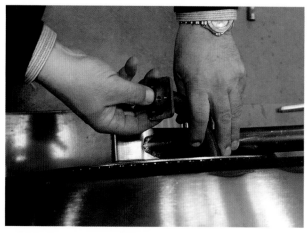

The tubular side mount seen here is a nice clean and sturdy way to mount the Perewitz license plate bracket.

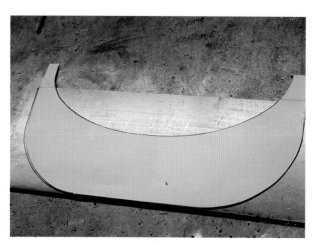

...it can be used to cut out the actual part from heavy steel plate.

"We like to get the license plate close to the pulley," explains David, "so it's out of the way."

The new part needs a little trimming before being welded to the fender.

Here it is, the mocked-up machine complete with seat pan, ready for disassembly.

cut. Jack cuts axle spacers from 6061 aluminum stock, explaining, "it cuts better than some of the other grades and it polishes better." Now Ron and Jack can reinstall the rear wheel with the newly cut axle spacers. Ron sets the fender on the tire after the rear wheel is positioned correctly. Next he makes a template of the front support plate - from 3/16 inch steel plate. The Perewitz license plate bracket will be mounted chopper fashion, on the left side. The exhaust pipes are from Samson, "we will probably have to make a bracket off the lower frame rail," explains Ron. "Because these are designed for a softail chassis."

Part two, Final Assembly

At this point the bike is ready for final assembly. The frame and fender are molded and painted with PPG candy orange. All the necessary parts have been ordered and delivered. Normally, most of the assemblies done at David's shop are the work of George Korey, but to speed things up Ron and Jack pitch in to help.

Part of aligning the engine and transmission is the installation of the BDL engine/transmission plate.

Once the painted frame is set on the work table, the first step is the installation of the engine and transmission.

This transmission is different than that used for mockup, the bearing race must be removed from the transmission shaft before the engine/tranny plate is installed.

This frame is designed to have the spacer shown used between the engine and the inside of the inner primary or engine/transmission plate.

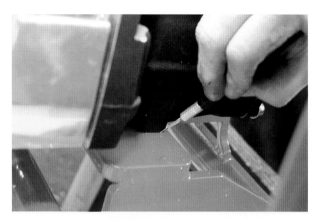

You can't have a big build up of paint under the engine and transmission. The area around the transmission is marked, then both units come out again...

The area on the inside of the frame shown here is raised like the engine mounting area, and the paint (which can be up to .030 inches thick) must be stripped off before the wheel is installed.

...so the paint can be removed from the area that was just marked. Redneck frames use raised areas where engine sits, which makes it easy to strip the paint off.

Paint sticks, available from tool supply houses, are used to put a thin layer of orange paint where the heavy paint build up was removed.

The oil tank straddles the tube, you have to take care that it floats correctly on the mounts and doesn't rub on the frame.

Once all the mounting areas are stripped of paint and touched up with the paint stick, the drivetrain can be re-installed.

The process starts as the engine and tranny are set in place temporarily. The inner primary bearing race must come off the transmission shaft before the BDL engine/transmission plate can be slipped in place.

The tranny mounting pad is slotted, George and Jack slide the transmission back and forth to align the transmission with the holes in the BDL engine/transmission plate. Once a couple of the bolts are screwed snug into the engine and transmission, Ronnie scribes the area around the transmission mounts (note the photos). Now the engine and transmission come back out so George can peel off the paint from the areas where the mounts will sit with an X-Acto knife and razor blade.

Meanwhile Jack installs the oil tank with blue Loctite on the bolts. The oil tank floats on the rubber mounts and it takes a certain amount of adjustment to get the oil tank to hang correctly in the frame without touching the center tube.

Now the engine and transmission can be set in the frame for the last time. The rear engine-mounting bolts don't want to drop down into the holes in the case because the cylinder fins protrude too far. The answer is to open up the holes slightly with a small die grinder. Now Jack and George install the engine/transmission support plate. "I like to use an O-ring between the engine case and the inside of the spacer," explains George, "because you get a better fit. In this case you don't need anything between the outer edge of the spacer and the inside of the plate."

George tightens the bolts that mount the engine/transmission plate for the last time. Now he can tighten the engine and transmission mounting bolts and studs.

TRIPLE TREES AND FRONT END

Before installing the stem and triple trees Ronnie cleans any over spray from the bearing races and the area just above and below the upper and lower races. It's also a good idea to check that the upper dust shield will fit over the lip on the outside of the neck.

The slotted plate, the female part of the fork

The fork stop is a two part affair. Part one is the slotted plate seen here, part two is the tabs on the bottom of the neck that interface with the slots.

Ron installs the stem (with red loctite) then the dust cap and the upper bearing, before dropping the whole affair into the neck.

A bolt with a tapered head comes up into the bottom of the lower tree to hold everything together. This is also the bolt that sets the adjustment of the stem bearings.

123

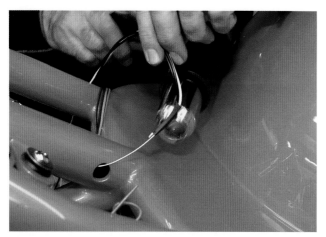

Thin welding rod is used as the "pull wire" to pull the various part of the harness through the frame. These wires will power the rear blinkers, and are pulled...

...all the way through the frame until they emerge at the very front.

Front end uses a one-sided brake made up of a GMA rotor and GMA 4-piston caliper.

stop, is affixed to the lower tree with four small machine screws (note photo, preceding page). The ProOne lower tree comes already tapped for these screws which Ron installs with a little blue Loctite. Red Loctite is placed on the threads of the stem before Ronnie screws it into the upper triple tree. Next he slides the dust cap and bearing on to the stem, then the upper tree with bars are set down on to the frame. Now Ron slips the lower bearing up onto the shaft, (no dust cap or seal on the bottom) then the lower tree and the tapered bolt that holds it all together. The adjustment of the bearings will be checked later when the tubes and wheel are in place.

WIRING

Each handle bar control from Custom Chrome includes two switches, each switch has two wires for a total of four per side. George uses an ohm-meter to determine which two wires go to each of the switches (note photos). Unfortunately, since the time the bike was mocked-up, David has decided to add blinker lights, so additional wires need to be added to the harness and pulled through the top tube.

At this point George has already run a basic harness through the frame. When David explains that the bike will have blinkers, however, George makes up an additional harness with three wires and pulls it through the tube with a piece of welding rod, starting at the back and pulling it through all the way to the front. (note the photos).

FRONT AND REAR WHEELS

Ronnie bolts the GMA rotor to the front wheel hub, the bolts are coated with Loctite and tightened to 25 ft. lbs. Like the front, the rear rotor is bolted to the hub with Loctite-coated bolts. The bolts are bigger (3/8 inch) and are tightened to 30-45 ft. lbs. The pulley is installed at the same time, and these bolts are tightened to 65 to 70 ft. lbs.

MORE WIRING

The harness for the HI 4 ignition starts out as five wires but there is no tachometer, and no VOES switch used on this bike, so it ends up as

Ron installs the front wheel...

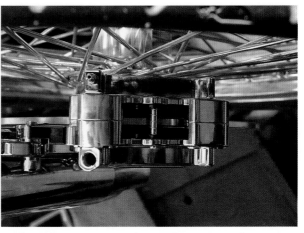

...the caliper is centered over the rotor as shown.

...per the details in the service manual.

As explained in the text, the ignition harness is made up of 3 wires, which are enclosed in shrink wrap before being...

Calipers should be installed with the bolts that come with the kit. Spacers are used between the caliper and the mount so...

...fished up the center tube and across the main tube with another piece of welding rod.

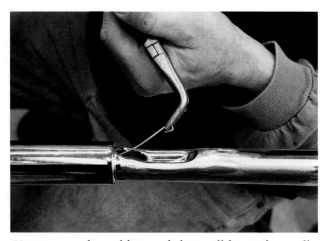

You can see the welding rod that will be used to pull the wires from the handle bar controls through the bars.

Each switch has two wires and each two-wire group is run through shrink wrap before being pulled through the bars.

Here the two, two-wire harnesses are pulled out the bottom of the bars.

only three wires. George extends the harness and runs it up the center tube, then over into the top tube, and up to the motor mount area. Once he has the wires hanging out from the tube, George slides the three wires, plus one additional wire, into a pieced of shrink wrap.

Most bike-building shops make up their harnesses from scratch. "Each bike is so different," explains David, "some have blinkers and some don't, some use handlebar switches and some don't." Making up a harness from scratch is probably beyond the capability of first time builders, however. For those individuals a harness kit from Thunder Heart or Wires Plus is probably a better answer. Some of these come in different "models" with and without provision for blinkers, for example.

Two more comments need to made regarding the wiring of your new ride. First, there's nothing that will put your bike on the side of the road quicker that an electrical malady. When the bike dies, or the headlight refuses to light, you're left with a mysterious problem that's hard to diagnose, especially out on the street somewhere. So (comment number two), electrical work needs to be of the highest quality. If you aren't comfortable making up a harness, buy one. If you're not comfortable installing the wiring harness, ask for help from your local motorcycle shop.

Ronnie runs two pieces of welding rod up through the bottom of the integral risers to the bar itself and over to each side. Jack drills a hole in one of the riser bolts, the wires for the handle bar switches will pass through this hollow bolt.

The wires from each switch assembly are grouped into two "harnesses," and slipped into shrink wrap, prior to mounting the controls on the bars.

Two circuit breakers are mounted just ahead of the rear fender, one 15 and one 30 amp. George installs the starter at this point, mostly so he knows how the starter wire should be routed.

Ronnie slips a piece of shrink-wrap tubing on the wires that go to the license plate and uses another piece of light welding rod to pull them

Jack uses a lathe to cut the hole in the center of the riser mounting bolt, "the key is to use lots of lubrication."

Eventually, the wires from the handle bars will be connected to those from the main harness...

Just making sure there's room for all the wires to come through the bolt.

...inside the headlight bucket.

Tightening the Allen bolt requires a specially hollowed out wrench.

Before screwing a bolt (especially a chrome one) into a chrome hub "you absolutely must chase the threads with a tap. Otherwise they'll gall in there for sure."

Now it's time to reinstall the rear wheel and 135 tooth belt.

Rear blinkers are bolted to the axle cover plates. Wires run up through the frame to the main harness.

Look close. The harnesses, from the main tube and the bars, are grouped inside a piece of stainless. Each end of the braided stainless is then slipped into a piece of shrink wrap. The effect is both durable and very neat.

through the tubing to the area under the seat.

The same procedure is followed for the bars. Using the same light welding rod Ronnie pulls the harnesses for the switches through the bars and down to the bottom of the left side riser.

INSTALL REAR PULLEY AND BRAKE ROTOR

"You absolutely have to tap the threads in a chrome hub like that," says Jack, "or for sure you will gall the bolt. And I use the tap dry, because any cutting oil you use will interfere with the Loctite. When you're trying to figure out how long the bolt should be, or how much bolt should engage in the female threads like this hub, the rule of thumb is: two times the diameter. For a quarter inch hole you should have a half-inch of thread engagement, any more than that and you're not adding to the strength."

The battery and tray slide in from underneath, (not shown) but the fit is so tight there isn't room for a standard soft-tail battery. In order to use a standard size battery Ron cuts the extra threads off the transmission mounting studs, and trims the tab for the "fifth transmission stud."

REAR BLINKERS/MORE HEADLIGHT AND HANDLEBAR WIRING

The rear turn signals are mounted to the axle cover plates, which requires drilling a hole up from the axle cavity into the upper tube on either side so the wires can pass out of sight to the main harness.

George runs the wires from the handlebars into a piece of stainless braid with shrink wrap on either end. The harness from the bike emerges at the front of the neck and into another piece of stainless with shrink wrap on either end. The headlight bucket seems the ideal place to connect the two harnesses. George drills two holes in the headlight bucket (and another for the hi-low switch), puts a grommet in each one and runs each harness into the bucket. (note the photo on the facing page).

A special tool is needed to tighten the crimp-style hose clamps.

OIL HOSES

The oil hoses are cut from bulk 5/16 inch I.D. bulk hose. For the stainless look you could either use bulk hose that's already wrapped, or use bulk stainless wrap slipped over each hose. The clamps are crimp-style (rather than screw-style) because they're neater. Routing is per the service manual.

THE FINAL BITS AND PIECES

The bike is almost finished, at this point Ronnie installs the forward controls, though he cleans the threads in the frame first. A little blue Loctite is applied to the bolts to ensure they won't back out, then the linkage rod is adjusted so the lever ends up in a comfortable position for the rider. Next, George finishes up the wiring and mounts the coils and switch assembly to the coil bracket.

The paint build up adds to the dimensions of all the parts, after paint the tank still drops onto the mounts but the fit is tight.

The regulator bolts to a chrome bracket (that did not come with the frame) mounted below the frame cross-member. Regulator base must have a good ground.

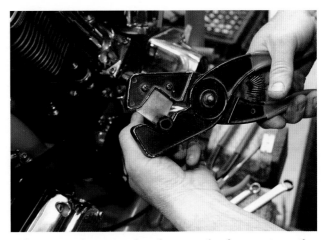

The cutter shown makes short work of trimming oil hoses to length.

129

Soldering How To

Soldering, and being able to make up a neat jumper wire, are necessary skills for anyone building a bike. After stripping off the insulation the first step is a dip in some non-acid flux.

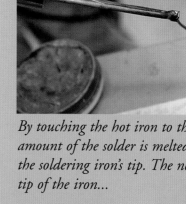

By touching the hot iron to the solder, a small amount of the solder is melted and drawn up onto the soldering iron's tip. The next step is to touch the tip of the iron...

Next, slide a small piece of shrink wrap onto the wire, followed by the connector.

...up against the connector. You don't want to just drop solder on, the connector needs to get hot enough that solder is drawn down into the connection.

Using a good crimp tool, crimp the connector onto the wire.

Slide the shrink wrap up over the connection, apply heat and bingo, you have a neat, insulated and durable connection.

Before attaching the forward controls, all the threads in the frame bungs must be chased to eliminate paint and debris.

BELT DRIVE

As mentioned, the belt drive is from BDL. The starter drive used with this set up is different than that used with a chain-primary. George installs the drive with one long Allen bolt coated with Red Loctite. Because of their experience with these starter arrangements, George and Jack make a few modifications to the starter-drive. "Sometimes the drive doesn't want to slide into the support bearing," explains George, "so we put a little taper on the end of the starter drive and a little chamfer on the support bushing."

The two belt pulleys have to be aligned, much like a chain primary, but with less tolerance for mis-alignment, "I try to get them perfectly aligned with a straight edge," explains George. "Otherwise the belt will walk up against

Ignition wiring is per the schematic that comes with the engine. Coils and switches mount to the Perewitz coil bracket. Dave uses an ignition and starter switch.

Starter drive comes with the BDL belt drive. Collar on right slides into end of shaft, both the end of the collar and end of the shaft are tapered slightly.

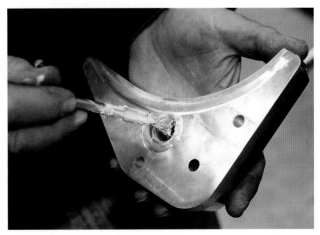

So the drive will slip into the support hole in the bracket. They also put a chamfer on the hole, and then lubricate before installation.

131

Above. As shown, spacers are used behind the drive sprocket to get the two sprockets aligned.

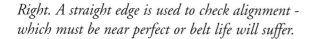

Right. A straight edge is used to check alignment - which must be near perfect or belt life will suffer.

The alignment should be double checked after the two nuts that hold on the sprockets are installed.

the outer pulley edge and self destruct."

Once the two pulleys are aligned by using the correct spacers behind the drive pulley, George finishes the installation of the clutch assembly. "For the initial clutch adjustment I like to screw the center stud in until it touches the clutch-release rod, then back it out about a quarter turn and then tighten the lock nut." The rest of the belt assembly is better described by the materials that come from the manufacturer.

The nut that holds on the clutch basket has left hand threads and is installed with a bit of red Loctite on the threads.

The seat is installed with a clip on the front...

George installs the rest of the clutch assembly. The nut in the center of the hub is turned in until it touches the clutch release shaft, then backed off about 1/4 turn.

...and an Allen bolt in the rear that screws down into a nut welded in place earlier. Be sure this bolt doesn't reach past the nut or it could contact the tire (ouch).

It isn't always cool to install the belt guard, but if the bike falls on you that spinning belt can cut a hole in your leg in short order.

A variety of junction blocks, with brackets, (the place to mount the brake light switch) are available to mount in the center of the bike.

To make the bike legal, a small horn is hidden under the seat.

LAST MINUTE DETAILS

The rear brake line is routed from the master cylinder to a junction block bolted to the transmission and on to the rear caliper. The brake light pressure switch is installed at the junction block.

The exhaust goes on now, using separate kits with flanges and gaskets.

George adds oil to the tank, "I put in 2-1/2 quarts to start with."

Ron attaches the front brake line to the upper tree with a small clamp, after drilling and tapping a hole in the tree (the brakes were bled later).

The finished machine definitely has the right stance and attitude for a chopper. And though you could build a similar bike for even less, the parts used here are a good value, inexpensive without sacrificing quality. What you might call an "almost cheap chopper."

The pipes are from Samson, the rear mounting tab was added during the mock-up.

134

With the exception of the paint, this is one cool chopper for less than twenty thousand dollars.

Big twin engine, 250 rear tire, hardtail frame, 21 inch front wheel, straight pipes, single down-tube frame and disc brakes. All the right stuff in other words.

Chapter Eleven

E-Z Choppa

Cheap Chopper Kit from Biker's Choice

Story and Photos by Alan Mayes

There are several options available to the average Joe looking to get into a new custom motorcycle. Buy a bike built by one of the many custom manufacturers out there. Though the bike is "custom," it may actually be like several hundred others except for some paint details. For a high quality unit like this, expect to pay $25,000 or more.

Another option: design the bike yourself and

This is not the bike from the assembly, but another E-Z Choppa after paint and assembly. One of the good things about a kit is the simple fact that you know before starting what the bike is going to look like when it's finished.

have a custom bike builder fabricate and build the bike for you. It will be unique, but it will be very costly. For this option, $50,000 or more is not an unusual price.

Option three, build it yourself. Either gather all the components from various catalogs and try to make them fit each other (they probably won't), or buy a kit bike. The problem with some so-called kit bikes is that the sellers of these kits have sometimes done what you would do, gather parts from various catalogs and hope they will all fit together. They often don't fit well, and the new owner is left with the task of trying to make something of all this assorted paraphernalia. This can be daunting for the novice bike builder and he often gives up. The upside of that scenario is that someone else might get to buy that abandoned "kit" for a bargain price when the first owner quits.

The guys at Biker's Choice say they have a better idea: kit bikes that actually fit together like a good kit should. Called Bike-in-a-Box, there are actually three models. The Desperado is reminiscent of a Harley FL, sans bags and windshield, but Softail-style. The Big Easy has more of a Softail Standard look. The third and most pop-

To make the whole job go more quickly, the engine (96 inch S&S) and transmission (a Delkron 5-speed) were already installed in the frame.

Once the triple trees are attached, Tommy Todd slips a tube assembly in place so George can attach the top nut.

Things start to take shape quickly with the addition of the wheels, bars and oil tank.

The transmission side cover comes off so Tommy can hook up the clutch cable.

All the brackets, including this upper motor-mount bracket, are already in place and drilled.

Forward controls and brake lines are next.

Though the 96 inch S&S engine comes complete, George and Tommy do have to install the S&S Shorty carburetor.

With a new gasket in place, Tommy installs the upper exhaust pipe.

ular version is the E-Z Choppa.

Skeeter Todd has done most of the work in sourcing the components for the Bikes-in-a-Box. He went to great pains to make sure that things actually fit together and many of the components are designed just for these bikes. The frames are made to Skeeter's specifications. The engines are 96" S&S models, other brand-name components include Corbin seats, Perewitz tanks, Excel wheels and Avon tires. In other words, these kits have high quality components from manufacturers we've actually heard of. Biker's Choice claims all you have to provide is paint and gas. Cables, wires, and everything else are provided. Retail prices range from $14,596 to $14,798.

All that is well and good, but the telling in a kit bike is how well it goes together. Skeeter and the boys acknowledge the skeptic in us all, so they offered to build one of the E-Z Choppa kits while we caught the whole build on film. Tommy Todd and George Morrow were the guys chosen to build the bike while we snapped away. The build took place in Indianapolis during the Annual Dealer Expo. So besides this photog-

Exhaust pipes go on next. All the mounting tabs for things like exhaust and sheet metal are already in place – and everything fits.

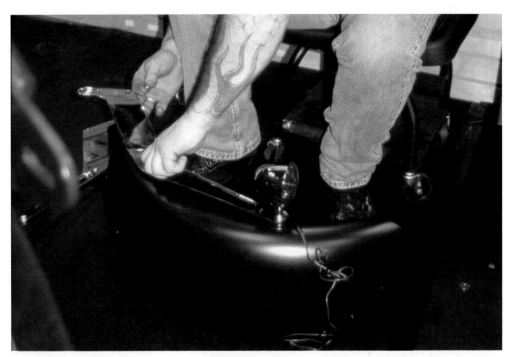

The front fender is a pretty simple bolt-on deal, the rear however, requires installation of the chrome struts and the lights.

Tommy works on the brake line routing while George installs the throttle cables and right side control.

At this point most of the harness is installed, clutch and throttle cables are run and the rear brake line is run.

E-Z Choppa uses conventional handlebar switches. The switches for each side have the harnesses already attached.

George installs rubber grommets in the mounting holes on the "Sportster" tank before bolting it onto the bike.

Biker's Choice includes chrome inner and outer primary, and a complete chain-style primary drive, with each kit.

Each kit comes complete with a solo-style Corbin seat.

rapher, there were a few thousand other motorcycle experts watching, too.

When the designated assemblers started the build, the only parts that were already staged were the engine and transmission case in the frame. That's it. The gears weren't even in the tranny. Other pieces like the lights, fender, controls, and so on, were hanging on the wall, still in their shrink pack. Five hours later, five people lifted an assembled motorcycle off the stand and rolled it away. It was completely assembled except for the wiring. Granted, Tommy and George had done this before, so they knew what they were doing, but this particular bike had never been assembled before. Yet, it fit together almost perfectly. The only finessing we saw involved a few strokes of a round file in a couple of mounting holes. Pretty impressive in our book.

Biker's Choice recommends that the customer have a professional shop, such as the one the kit was purchased from, assemble the bike. It looked to us though that a mechanically able customer could probably do it himself. Probably in

The 41mm front end uses chrome lower legs, extended tubes and a single disc. Note the brake line, all the hoses and lines are braided stainless.

two or three weekends, it went together that smoothly. Rather than provide an assembly manual for the kit, just use a Harley Davidson factory shop manual for a softail.

Five hours after starting the bike is finished and ready to run.

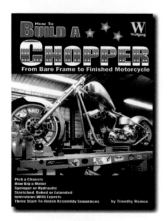

HOW TO BUILD A CHOPPER

Designed to help you build your own chopper, this book covers History, Frames, Chassis Components, Wheels and Tires, Engine Options, Drivetrains, Wiring, Sheet Metal and Hardware. Included are assembly sequences from the Arlen Ness, Donnie Smith and American Thunder shops. Your best first step! Order today.

Choppers are back! Learn from the best how to build yours.
12 chapters cover:
- Use of Evo, TC, Shovel, Pan or Knucklehead engines
- Frame and running gear choices
- Design decisions - short and stubby or long and radical?
- Four, five or six-speed trannies

Twelve Chapters	144 Pages	$24.95	Over 300 photos-over 50% color

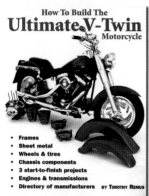

BUILD THE ULTIMATE V-TWIN MOTORCYCLE

An explosion of new parts from the motorcycle aftermarket now makes it possible to build your own motorcycle from scratch. One designed from the start to answer your need for speed and style. This book is intended to help you make intelligent choices from among the vast number of frames, engines and accessories available today.

You can assemble all those parts into a running motorcycle with tips from men who build bikes professionally. Learn which is the best wiring harness or transmission and the best way to install those parts on your new bike.

After designing, choosing and assembling, all that's left is the registration and insurance. From the first concept to the final bolt, from dream to reality. Yes, you can build your own motorcycle.

Ten Chapters	144 Pages	$19.95	Over 250 photos

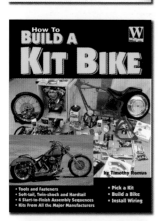

HOW TO BUILD A KIT BIKE

How To Build a Kit Bike explains how to choose the best kit and then assemble those parts into a complete running motorcycle. See bikes built in the shops of: Cory Ness, Kendall Johnson and American Thunder. If you own a kit or plan to buy a kit bike, this is the book you need — designed to help you turn that pile of parts into your own very cool motorcycle.

Eight chapters with 300+ photos & illustrations.
- Tools and Fasteners
- Soft-tail, Twin-shock and Hardtail
- 4 Start-to-Finish Assembly Sequences
- Kits From All The Major Manufacturers

Eight Chapters	144 Pages	$24.95	Over 300 photos, 60% color

ADVANCED CUSTOM PAINTING TECHNIQUES

When it comes to custom painting, there is one name better known than all the others, and that name is Jon Kosmoski. Whether the project in your shop rides on two wheels or four, whether you're trying to do a simple kandy job or complex graphics, this how-to book from Jon Kosmoski is sure to answer your questions. Chapters one through three cover Shop Equipment, Gun Control and Paint Materials. Chapters four through seven get to the heart of the matter with complete start-to-finish painting sequences.
- Shop set up
- Gun Control
- Use of new paint materials
- 4 start-to-finish sequences
- Two wheels or four
- Simple or complex
- Kandy & Klear

Seven Chapters	144 Pages	$24.95	Over 350 photos, 100% color

More Great Books From Wolfgang Publications!
http://www.wolfgangpublications.com

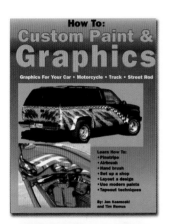

HOW TO: CUSTOM PAINT & GRAPHICS

A joint effort of the master of custom painting, Jon Kosmoski and Tim Remus, this is the book for anyone who wants to try their hand at dressing up their street rod, truck or motorcycle with lettering, flames or exotic graphics. A great companion to Kustom Painting Secrets (below).

7 chapters include:
• Shop tools and equipment
• Paint and materials
• Letter & pinstripe by hand
• Design and tapeouts
• Airbrushing
• Hands-on, Flames and signs
• Hands-on, Graphics

| Seven Chapters | 144 Pages | $24.95 | Over 250 photos, 50% in color |

KUSTOM PAINTING SECRETS

More from the master! From the basics to advanced custom painting tricks, Jon Kosmoski shares his 30 years of experience in this book. Photos by publisher Tim Remus bring Jon's text to life. A must for anyone interested in the art of custom painting.

7 chapters include:
• History of House of Kolor
• How to set up a shop
• Color painting sequences
• Prepare for paint
• Final paint application
• Hands-on, basic paint jobs
• Hands-on, beyond basic paint
• Hands-on, custom painting

| Seven Chapters | 128 Pages | $19.95 | 250 photos with color section |

ULTIMATE SHEET METAL FABRICATION

In an age when most products are made by the thousands, many yearn for the one-of-kind metal creation. Whether you're building or restoring a car, motorcycle, airplane or (you get the idea), you'll find the information you need to custom build your own parts from steel or aluminum.

11 chapters include:
• Lay out a project
• Pick the right material
• Shrinkers & stretchers
• English wheel
• Make & use simple tooling
• Weld aluminum or steel
• Use hand and power tools

| Eleven Chapters | 144 Pages | $19.95 | Over 350 photos |

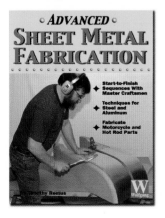

ADVANCED SHEET METAL FABRICATION

Advanced Sheet Metal Fabrication Techniques, is a photo-intensive how-to book. See Craig Naff build a Rolls Royce fender, Rob Roehl create a motorcycle gas tank, Ron Covell form part of a quarter midget body and Fay Butler shape an aircraft wheel fairing. Methods and tools include English wheel, power hammer, shrinkers and stretchers, and of course the hammer and dolly.

• Sequences in aluminum and steel
• Multi-piece projects
• Start to finish sequences
• From building the buck to shaping the steel
• Includes interviews with the metal shapers
• Automotive, motorcycle and aircraft

| 7 Chapters | 144 Pages | $24.95 | 144 pages, over 300 photos - 60% color |

Sources

American Thunder
16760 Toronto Ave.
Prior Lake, MN 55372
1.877.389.0138
952.226.1180

Biker's Choice
Dealer Info Line: 800.343.9687
www.bikerschoice.com

Klock Werks
915 South Kimball
Mitchell, SD 57301-4405
605.996.3700
www.kustomcycles.com

Motorcycle Works
213 W. Dennis
Olathe, Kansas 66061
913.768.6888

Mike's Choppers
www.mikeschoppers.com
Handmade Metric frames

Perse Performance
www.perseperformance.com

Precison Metal Fabrication (PMFR)
589 Citation Dr.
Shakopee, MN 55379
952.496.0053

Down by Law Custom Cycles
Ken Kuhnke
www.cyclexchange.net
Honda frames and chopper parts
715.356.7346

Redneck Engineering
107 Nix Rd.
Liberty, SC 29657
864.843.3001

Savage Custom Motorcycle
Savage, Minnesota
Steve Tersteeg
612.382.4500

Shadley Brothers/Auto Tec
1125 Bedford, Route 18
Whitman, MA 02382
781.447.2403

Lowriders by Summers
Tom Summers
612.824.8777

Perewitz Motorcycles
Cycle Fabrications
910 Plymouth Street
Bridgewater, Massachusetts 02324
508-697-3595
Perewitz, Dave
www.perewitz.com